D1558939

DISASTER!

RIVERGATE REGIONALS

Rivergate Regionals is a collection of books published by Rutgers University Press focusing on New Jersey and the surrounding area. Since its founding in 1936, Rutgers University Press has been devoted to serving the people of New Jersey, and this collection solidifies that tradition. The books in the Rivergate Regionals Collection explore history, politics, nature and the environment, recreation, sports, health and medicine, and the arts. By incorporating the collection within the larger Rutgers University Press editorial program, the Rivergate Regionals Collection enhances our commitment to publishing the best books about our great state and the surrounding region.

DISASTER!

Stories of Destruction and Death in Nineteenth-Century New Jersey

ALAN A. SIEGEL

RUTGERS UNIVERSITY PRESS

NEW BRUNSWICK, NEW JERSEY, AND LONDON

Library of Congress Cataloging-in-Publication Data
Siegel, Alan A., 1939–
    Disaster! : stories of destruction and death in nineteenth-century New Jersey /
Alan A. Siegel.
        pages cm. — (Rivergate Regionals)
    Includes bibliographical references and index.
    ISBN 978–0–8135–6459–3 (hardcover : alk. paper) — ISBN 978–0–8135–6460–9
(e-book)
    1. Natural disasters—New Jersey—History. 2. Disasters—New Jersey—History.
3. Natural disasters—New Jersey—Anecdotes. 4. Disasters—New Jersey—Anecdotes.
I. Title.
    GB5010.S478 2014
    363.3409749'09034—dc23

                                                                    2013010368

A British Cataloging-in-Publication record for this book is available from the British
Library.

Copyright © 2014 by Alan A. Siegel

All rights reserved

No part of this book may be reproduced or utilized in any form or by any means,
electronic or mechanical, or by any information storage and retrieval system, without
written permission from the publisher. Please contact Rutgers University Press, 106
Somerset Street, New Brunswick, NJ 08901. The only exception to this prohibition is
"fair use" as defined by U.S. copyright law.

Visit our website: http://rutgerspress.rutgers.edu

Manufactured in the United States of America

CONTENTS

DISASTER!

INTRODUCTION

By every measure, Hurricane Sandy was a disaster of epic proportion. The deadliest storm to strike the East Coast since Hurricane Diane in 1955, Sandy killed thirty-seven people and caused more than $30 billion in damage to New Jersey alone. Overall, twenty-four states suffered the effects of the hurricane, a one thousand-mile-wide monster that came ashore near Atlantic City just after 8:00 P.M. on October 29, 2012. Superstorm Sandy will live on in the collective memory of New Jerseyans—and will be written about, too—for decades to come.

People have been fascinated by disasters like Hurricane Sandy since the time of the Flood, if not before. We know this because almost all cultures tell ancient stories of a catastrophic deluge that overwhelmed the land and annihilated the people. Such narratives are common in India, China, Polynesia, Turkey, the Baltic countries, and South America, to name just a few. The Greeks cherished the tale of Deucalion, son of Prometheus and mythical ancestor of the Hellenes, who built a boat and thereby thwarted Zeus, who had threatened to destroy mankind by a flood. The biblical story of Noah and his ark is universally known. Even older is the epic of Gilgamesh, the king whose ancestor had braved not only a black cloud that "turned all light to darkness" but a cyclone and flood that "devastated the land" as well.

Natural disasters—hurricanes, floods, earthquakes, and volcanic eruptions—were the stuff of legend. In the modern age, manmade calamities—shipwrecks, fires, train wrecks, and airplane crashes—are more common. Regardless of the cause, people are captivated by stories of such great events.

Why do we have such an interest in death and destruction? Natural curiosity plays a large role; after all, most of us thankfully will never experience a shipwreck or flood except vicariously through news reports, books, and television shows. Are we relieved that we have escaped to live another day? Do we feel compassion for the survivors or admiration for the bravery and selflessness of people facing the gravest dangers? No doubt a variety of motives draws people inexorably to stories of disasters.

In the nineteenth century, news reports of calamities provided common fodder for newspapers, increasing circulation by the thousands. James Gordon Bennett, who founded the *New York Herald* in 1835, was among the pioneers of journalism as we know it. His paper's vivid and detailed account of the New York City fire of December 1835 set a standard by which disaster reporting would be measured.

In the following pages, I tell the stories of more than a score of natural and manmade disasters that befell the people of New Jersey in the nineteenth century.* My sources for the most part are contemporary newspaper accounts; as far as I know, no one has collected these mostly long-forgotten accounts together in one book. And wherever possible, I have consciously emphasized the roles played by those who, faced with sudden disaster, performed heroically. None of the stories end well—there are dead and injured by the thousands, as well as millions of dollars in property losses. Still, we cannot but admire the courage of those who experienced firsthand such calamities and survived to tell the tale.

* Three of the disasters I write about occurred in the opening years of the twentieth century. I include them because they are related to similar events that took place before the turn of the century.

CHAPTER 1

FIRES

From the beginning of recorded human history, fire has been both comforter and destroyer. The terrible conflagrations that leveled Rome in A.D. 64 and London in September 1666 are but two examples of the destructive force of one of nature's most terrifying elements.

In nineteenth-century urban America, when many buildings were close-packed, ramshackle wooden structures, the warmth of the fireplace and wood stove and the light of the oil and gas lamp were decidedly mixed blessings. It took but one careless moment to set a building ablaze. With fire brigades usually nonexistent or poorly staffed and equipped, the orange glow of an unconfined flame could spread at frightening speed, destroying lives and property indiscriminately until burning out of its own accord.

Even today, with all of our modern firefighting methods, fire takes a heavy toll. In the United States, property loss resulting from residential fires alone in the three-year period ending in 2008 amounted to $6.92 billion; during the same period, nearly fifteen thousand civilians died or were injured in those blazes. Even a state as well protected as New Jersey has not been spared: fire fatalities in the year 2010, the last for which statistics are currently available, totaled 73, with 393 injuries. That year, there were 30,841 fires statewide. Losses were in the millions.

Newark—October 27, 1836

New Jersey's first great fire struck Newark on a cold afternoon, October 27, 1836. It was a few minutes after three o'clock when a lodger in a German boarding house on East Market Street first discovered the flames. Within minutes, the old two-story, wood-frame structure was a roaring inferno. Moments later, the adjacent frame buildings on the east and west, and sheds to the rear, were burning furiously. Soon rows of shops on both sides of Mechanic Street were ablaze, with flying embers carrying the fire quickly to a three-story carriage factory on the corner of Broad Street. The fire raged up Broad, consuming factories, shops, and fine old homes, until it met the flames burning along Market Street. In less than three hours, an entire city block bounded by Broad, Mechanic, Mulberry, and Market Streets was engulfed.

The five Newark fire companies that responded to the first cries of "Fire!" found their efforts crippled by a lack of water and bursting hoses. Hundreds of citizens pitched in to help the fire laddies, but when it became apparent that the fire could not be stopped, all efforts turned to the rescue of property in the path of the flames. Volunteers frantically emptied houses, offices, factories, and sheds of their contents, jumbling furniture, bedding, clothing, machinery, and merchandise in mid-street.

Firemen from Rahway, Elizabeth, Belleville, and New York City—which dispatched six companies by ferry and railroad flatcar—responded to Newark's frantic calls for help to "battle bravely with the demon of devastation," as one writer put it. Only through superhuman effort were firemen able to save two of Newark's landmarks, the venerable First Presbyterian Church (its vestry building was badly scorched) and a fireproof two-story brick building on the corner of Mechanic and Broad Streets occupied by the State Bank. A garden between the bank building and the approaching flames acted as a natural firebreak.

Hurrying to Newark with the Elizabeth fire companies, two naval officers, Captain Gedney of the U.S. surveying schooner *New-Jersey* and

Lieutenant Dayton Williamson, volunteered to check the fire's spread by blowing up buildings in its path. A frantic search for sufficient gunpowder proved futile, however, and for five hours the fire continued its work of devastation, incinerating Captain Gillespie's Washington Hotel, a new four-story, fireproof brick building, along with chandlery, clothing, and millinery shops, grocery stores, carriage factories, a brass foundry, workshops, sheds, offices, factories, rooming houses occupied mostly by poor families, and private dwellings—in all, nearly fifty structures, several of them substantial. According to the *Newark Daily Advertiser*, the losses totaled $120,000, a goodly sum in those days, only $75,000 of which was insured.* Fortunately, there were no fatalities.

"Great apprehensions were excited at one time that the whole eastern side of the city would be destroyed," reported the *Daily Advertiser*, "but it was preserved, and great as the calamity is, there is still great cause for thankfulness for the protecting care of a merciful Providence." At the height of the fire, showers of sparks kindled blazes at several points north of Market Street, but the vigilance of volunteers who stationed themselves on rooftops and in backyards with buckets of water prevented the flames from spreading beyond the city block already involved. "One case of intrepidity and generous self-sacrifice deserves special mention," said the *Advertiser*. "Alexander Kirkpatrick, a journeyman Mechanic, signalized himself in saving Asa Torrey's house, upon the roof of which he was sometime exposed to the billowy sheets of flame from the adjoining building, pouring water from buckets handed through the scuttle, at the peril of his life." Kirkpatrick, as modest as he was heroic, declined to accept a "handsome fee" offered as a reward for saving Torrey's brick home. Another intrepid soul, unfortunately anonymous, dashed into a burning building

* Throughout this book, damages are reported in contemporary dollars. There is no easy way to translate an 1836 dollar loss, for example, into present-day values. One well-regarded tool can be found at Measuring Worth.com (http://www.measuring -worth.com/calculators/uscompare/result.php). Using its calculator, the Newark fire caused a loss of $3 million in 2012 dollars. The owners of the *Vizcaya*, which sank in 1890, suffered a $12.8 million loss.

to save an eleven-year-old boy stranded on a blazing rooftop. Cradling the boy in his arms, the man jumped two flights to the ground, deposited the boy on the street unharmed and disappeared into the cheering crowd.

The day after the fire, Newark's *Daily Advertiser* attempted to put the best face it could on the city's greatest calamity. "A large number of workmen have been turned out of employ, and there must be a temporary suspension of a great amount of business, but on the whole there is great reason for thankfulness, that so many of the sufferers will be able to sustain themselves," said the paper. "It is not probable that so extensive a fire could have occurred in any other portion of the city, though the burnt district is comprised in the very centre of business, with less suffering. There are some individual cases where the evil will be sorely felt, but the largest portion of the buildings destroyed were old frame workshops and warehouses, from which the personal property was chiefly rescued, and but few families have been turned out of doors." The truth, unfortunately, was that Newark's twenty thousand people were just then falling victim to a nationwide manufacturing depression that would culminate in the Panic of 1837. Thousands of workmen were soon thrown out of work, joining those burned out in the fire of 1836. Many of the charred factories and shops south of Broad Street lay in ruin for years.

Cape May City—September 5, 1856

Cape May City's claim as America's oldest seaside resort dates to 1801, when Ellis Hughes, who owned a tavern and hotel, advertised in the Philadelphia newspapers a night's lodging for seven cents. "The subscriber has prepared himself for entertaining company who use sea bathing," proclaimed Hughes, "and he is accommodated with extensive house room, with fish, oysters and crabs and good liquors." Cape May's popularity surged when the steamboat *General Jackson* began making regular weekly runs from Philadelphia to the cape in 1816. An added stop at New Castle, Delaware, opened the resort to passengers from the southern states, firmly establishing Cape May's reputation as a favorite playground for the wealthy seeking to escape the South's humid summers.

As the resort's popularity increased, entrepreneurs lavished thousands of dollars on ever larger wood-frame hotels, many of them enormous, ornate structures that could accommodate hundreds, and in some cases, thousands of guests. Henry Clay and Abraham Lincoln were two of the resort's earliest distinguished visitors. Clay's two-week stay in 1847 reinforced Cape May's position as the country's finest seaside resort. More numerous than the politicians were the planters from Delaware, Maryland, and Virginia, who rode their thoroughbred horses on the wide beaches during the day and spent the evenings gambling in the casinos.

Among Cape May's remarkable hotels, the most remarkable of all was the Mount Vernon, built by a company of Philadelphia investors at Broadway and Beach Avenues at a cost of $125,000. Said to be the largest hotel in the world, the Mount Vernon was simply immense. "Although the hotel . . . was capable of accommodating 2,100 visitors, it was not finished," reported the *New-York Daily Times*. "It was designed to . . . occupy three sides of a hollow square, or court yard, and the front range and one wing were up. . . . The building was constructed entirely of wood; it was four stories in height in the main, with four towers, each five stories in height. Three of these towers occupied the corners of the building, and one stood midway of the only wing. In addition to these towers there was an immense tower six stories in height in the centre of the front. The entire structure, both outside and upon the court-yard, was surrounded with wooden piazzas that extended from the ground to the roof, with floors at each story." The wing was five hundred feet in length, and the front extended another three hundred feet. "The dining room, which was 425 feet long and 60 feet wide, was capable of accommodating 3,000 persons. There were 432 rooms in the building . . . [with] stables for fifty horses, carriage houses, ten-pin alleys, etc." The Mount Vernon, said the paper, was "celebrated . . . for the superior accommodations the building offered its guests. The interior was well-finished, and the apartments were larger and more comfortable than usual at watering place hotels." Unique among early hostelries, the Mount Vernon boasted a bathroom in each room. The hotel's luxurious furnishings alone were valued at $94,000.

On the evening of Friday, September 5, 1856, the hotel's manager, sixty-five-year-old Philip Cain, and his family—sons Philip Jr. and Andrew, teenage daughters Martha and Sarah, and Mrs. Albertson, Cain's housekeeper—were alone in the hotel, or so they thought. Cain's wife and several other children were in nearby Vincentown, but the Mount Vernon's manager, a busy season just behind him, preferred the quiet of his magnificent hotel. No doubt, too, there was much work to be done before the hotel could be closed for the winter.

Shortly before eleven o'clock, after the family had retired for the night, fire broke out in three different places. Unable to escape, and overcome by the dense smoke, manager Cain, his two daughters, one son, and the housekeeper perished in the flames. Son Philip, although badly burned, saved himself by jumping from a second-story window. Within an hour's time, the Mount Vernon was a complete loss. Its buildings constructed almost entirely of wood, Cape May City was surprisingly unprepared for a fire, even a minor one: There was no fire apparatus of any kind for miles. Only because the Mount Vernon stood at a considerable distance from the resort's other hotels was the city saved from total ruin.

On the Monday following the fire, New Jersey newspapers reported that the wife of an Irishman who claimed Cain owed him $100 had been arrested and committed to jail on a charge of arson. "It is said that she had the day before, and up to late in [the] evening previous, been heard to utter the most serious threats against Mr. Cain."

Inexplicably, the loss of the Mount Vernon, and a fire that razed the Mansion House the following year, failed to alert Cape May's town leaders to the transparent need for a city fire department. Although the newer hotels were now equipped with their own water tanks, fire hoses, and employees trained to detect and fight fires, the resort was a tinderbox in search of a match. The United States Hotel, built in 1850 and one of the

Figure 1. Trumpeted as the largest hotel in the world when it was built in 1855–1856, Cape May's Mount Vernon boasted a bathroom in each of its 432 rooms and a dining room that seated three thousand. From *Frank Leslie's Illustrated Newspaper*, September 20, 1856.

largest and best equipped on the island, was the target of so many arson attempts that a vigilante force was established in 1863 to protect both the building and the town.

Cape May City—August 31, 1869

Disaster struck once again on August 31, 1869, the very year that President Ulysses S. Grant vacationed at the United States Hotel. It was 2:30 in the morning when the dreaded flames were first discovered flickering in a two-story building occupied by Peter Boyton, known locally as the Pearl Diver. Packed with flammable material, including Japanese paper kites and lanterns, lacquer boxes, and cotton goods, Boyton's shop was soon burning fiercely. A handful of would-be firefighters who, acting without direction, broke in windows and knocked down doors unintentionally vented the fire, which then spread relentlessly from one building to the next. The town's hook and ladder truck arrived, along with the mayor, W. B. Miller, who attempted to bring some order out of confusion, but the uncoordinated efforts of a thousand or more volunteers were no match for the fire, which had now gained an insurmountable headway. Unfortunately for the city, the wind, stirring only lightly when the fire began, now began to blow briskly toward the ocean, carrying sparks and flames to all of the buildings east of the Pearl Diver.

The United States Hotel, sold only the week before to a New York investor for $80,000, stood directly in the path of the fire, protected by a twenty-seven-thousand-gallon water tank and a corps of employees determined to save it. They hung wet blankets over the balconies facing nearby burning buildings and played almost all of their precious water on surrounding structures, but the intense heat and smoke proved too much for the hotel employees. Forced to retreat, they could only look on helplessly as the wooden structure first smoldered and then burst into flame. Wind-driven sparks soon ignited the American House and the New Atlantic Hotel, together with a score of lesser buildings in between. When it became clear that the United States Hotel was doomed, "the guests hurriedly poured out in a great crowd, men, women and children, scarcely clothed, and unnerved by fright," reported the *New York Times*. "Each person was burdened with such articles of personal property as he had been able to snatch up in the hurry and terror of the moment; men bore out trunks, and women and children struggled under unwieldy loads of clothing. But there was little time to save property, and hardly more than enough to make sure that no human being should be swallowed up in the hot fire."

After the United States Hotel caught fire, it was at once clear to everyone that no part of the city was safe. "The town was now thoroughly alarmed and aroused," continued the *Times*. "Every hotel, every house, every store was emptied of its inmates, who fled inland with such part of their portable property as they had been able to collect. Nor was the alarm groundless or the haste uncalled for. The flames spread with terrible rapidity." From the United States Hotel the blaze extended in almost every direction, ultimately devastating one-fourth of the city, consuming in its fury "the heart and beauty of the pleasant town." Several of Cape May's finest hotels were saved almost by chance: Congress Hall (where Lincoln once vacationed) was protected by a row of trees that refused to ignite; the LaPierre House escaped the flames when its owners tore up its carpets, dowsed them with water, and spread them on its roof; the Columbia House owed its preservation to the "almost superhuman exertions" of five employees who, wrapped in wet blankets, managed to cling to the rooftops of adjoining buildings, extinguishing every firebrand that threatened devastation.

"The escape of the Columbia House from destruction is looked upon as the most wonderful occurrence of this terrible drama," said the *Times*, "and is altogether owing to the clear foresightedness of two or three of its employees in tearing away some smaller out-buildings and in the judicious use of the hotel's supply of water. The scene from the roof of the Columbia was terrifically sublime. The red flames checked the fall of the frame buildings, and the large clouds of smoke, interspersed with sparks, floated out to sea, and hung like a pall above the surf." The three steam fire engines from Camden that arrived by special train at noon could do little more than hose down the smoldering ruins. Losses from the fire exceeded $300,000.

Unwilling to acknowledge that the town's sprawling wooden hotels might themselves be the cause of its troubles, Cape May searched for a culprit, convinced that the fire was of incendiary origin. Peter Boyton, the Pearl Diver, who had himself lost $1,000 in cash in the fire, was hauled before the mayor only to be discharged after a brief hearing that produced no proof that he was the arsonist. "There immediately followed a tremendous burst of applause from all present," reported the *Cape May Ocean Wave*, "a large proportion being ladies." A $1,000 reward offered by the mayor and City Council for the arrest and conviction of the incendiary

Figure 2. Losses exceeded $300,000 when another fire, said to be the work of an arsonist, swept through Cape May's hotel district in 1869. Courtesy of the Cape May County Historical and Genealogical Society.

proved ineffective. Cape May once again began to rebuild; within two years, all evidence of the fire had been erased.

Cape May City—November 9, 1878

A newspaperman writing in the 1870s called Cape May "the favorite watering place of Philadelphia." It was, he wrote, "a town with a population of about 3,000, which is increased to nearly 6,000 by the transient visitors of a summer season. The town is 81 miles from Philadelphia, on a point of land at the most remote portion of the southern extremity of New Jersey. The Town of Cape May is of itself not attractive, and the fashionable hotels are all built on what was formerly Cape Island, once separated from the mainland by a small creek that has been filled. Cape Island is about 250 acres in extent, and, besides the hotels, is occupied by numerous cottages." Among the twenty-four hotels, he wrote, the largest were the Stockton, Congress Hall, the Columbia, the Centre, and the Ocean House. "All these buildings were frame, and some of them were imposing in their proportions. . . . The popularity of the place as a resort area arises from the fact that it has an exposure on three sides to the ocean view, and an atmosphere which in summer always affords relief from the heated city. The only drawback comes from a northerly wind, which brings with it not only resinous odors but clouds of mosquitoes."

The era of Cape May's grand hotels came to a fiery end on the morning of November 9, 1878, when the resort city's third major conflagration in little more than twenty years broke out in the attic of the new wing of the Ocean House. Discovered by a policeman at seven in the morning, the fire burned through the day and was not brought under control until six in the evening, after it had laid waste forty acres of buildings. Burning over much of the same area destroyed in the 1869 blaze, the fire caused nearly $700,000 in damage, leveling the Ocean House; Congress Hall, one of the resort's finest hotels with accommodations for 1,200; the Atlantic, rebuilt on the site of its predecessor destroyed nine years earlier; and the Columbia House, one of the oldest on the island with rooms for 600. Of the resort's major hotels, only the Stockton, built at a cost of $600,000, survived, although it too was damaged by flames that came within feet of its magnificent porches.

Originally built in 1832, and renovated and enlarged in 1856, the Ocean House stood across Perry Street from Congress Hall's expansive lawn. Three hundred thirty feet long and three and a half stories in height, the Ocean House was surrounded by porches and balconies that provided splendid views of the beach and ocean. With 150 rooms that accommodated

Figure 3. Cape May's third major fire in twenty-two years laid waste forty acres of hotels, summer cottages, and businesses. Less than half of the loss was covered by insurance. Courtesy of the Cape May County Historical and Genealogical Society.

four hundred guests, Cape May's oldest hotel had been redecorated in the spring of 1877 at a cost of $80,000.

"The wind at the time the fire started was blowing a gale from the north-west," according to the *New York Times*, "and in a few moments the Ocean House became a mass of flames, which at once communicated to Congress Hall, one of the largest hotels in the place, on the opposite side of the street. The southern wing of this structure was quickly wrapped in a sheet of fire, and in half an hour the entire block of buildings on the

15

plot, with the exception of an old storehouse, was in ruins. This progress westward was gained against the wind. The flames from the Ocean House communicated, at the same time, to the Centre House, a large hotel adjoining Fryer's cottage, a handsome dwelling filled with works of art."

Cape May's fire department, equipped with a hand-operated engine with fifteen feet of rubber hose, a hook and ladder truck company, and three chemical engines, could do little in the face of a 35-mile-per-hour wind that blew without letup throughout the day. Earlier in the year, the fire chief's call for more funding had been denied owing to budget constraints. A bucket brigade manned by hotel staff and residents that stretched three hundred feet from Congress Hall to the ocean proved equally useless. Engine companies summoned by Mayor Thomas Edmunds from Camden, Vineland, and Philadelphia once again reached the city too late to be of any real assistance. After a steam fire engine that arrived by special train at midday from Camden helped check the flames at Perry and Jackson Streets, the wind blew the fire in another direction. "The roar of the flames was terrific, and the strong wind blew the burning embers before it in a perfect shower," reported a New York paper, "setting fire to whatever building they were deposited upon." The intense heat forced the firemen to fall back time and again; not until early morning, when the fire had nearly burned itself out, were they able to establish a line of defense along Ocean Street.

"The real wonder is, not at the size of the fire but that there has been so long an escape for a town so constructed and with no fire department worthy of the name," clucked the *Newark Daily Advertiser* the day after the fire. "Every one of those great hotels is a tinder box, needing hardly more than the application of a match to lead to a conflagration." Although the cause of the fire was never discovered, almost everyone agreed that it was arson. Its origin, said one newspaper, was "in the middle of a room in the Ocean House, where it could not be reached. Those who were first on the ground declare that they observed a strong odor of petroleum." The owner of the Ocean House, Samuel R. Ludlum, seen taking the early train for Philadelphia only fifteen minutes before the fire was discovered, was interrogated by authorities but promptly released for lack of evidence.

Seven railroad cars "well-filled with spectators and cottagers" arrived from Philadelphia just as the final embers were doused. What they saw was a town effectively burned to the ground. Once again the entire center was destroyed, most of the summer cottages were gone, and the business district was wrecked. The fire ruined not only the old resort but also, financially, many of the investors and property owners who had built there: less than half of the loss was covered by insurance. Although the town was eventually rebuilt, the new construction (some of it brick) was on a vastly reduced scale and took much longer to accomplish than did the rapid recovery after the 1869 fire. The Columbia House, the Atlantic Hotel, and the Ocean House were never replaced. The new Congress Hall was half the size of its burned-out namesake. Already in decline as New Jersey's most fashionable watering place, Cape May never fully recovered from what the New York Times called "the most destructive fire which has ever visited any sea-side resort."

The Cape May fire was not the only one to make headlines during the 1870s, a decade that severely challenged America's firefighters. Between October 1871 and December 1876, the country suffered five of the worst fires in its history. The first nearly destroyed Chicago, consuming 17,450 buildings, killing more than three hundred people, and causing estimated property losses of $200 million. On the same day, 250 miles north of the burning city, another fire broke out in the pine forests surrounding the small town of Peshtigo, this one eventually burning more than a million acres and killing another 1,200 people. Thirteen months later a fearful blaze devastated Boston's downtown area, turning a square mile of the city into ashes while claiming thirteen lives. Another twenty-two people died in December 1872 when New York City's Fifth Avenue Hotel caught fire. In December 1876, a horrific fire raced through a packed theater in Brooklyn, taking nearly three hundred lives in thirty minutes.

Newton—September 22, 1873

The county seat of Sussex County, Newton was a thriving village of 2,400 located on trade routes between Newark and parts west. Arrival of the Sussex Railroad in 1854 sparked a building boom that continued throughout the Civil War era. By 1870, Newton boasted a foundry, sash and blind factory, two carriage manufacturers, five churches, and about fifty stores clustered around the town green. Newton's two newest buildings were Samuel Johnson's dry goods store at the corner of Main and Spring Streets—a three-story brick structure built in the then-popular Second Empire style, where its owner sold men's and ladies' clothing, china, carpets, lighting fixtures, and sundry housewares—and the Library Building, a three-story pile of brick trimmed with blue limestone, also in the Second Empire style. A gift of Alfred L. Dennis, a Newton native who made his fortune as a Newark bookseller and railroad executive, the $25,000 building housed retail space, a library, and on the third floor a five-hundred-seat auditorium. The builders claimed that both structures were fireproof. Between Johnson's store and the library stood seven brick-and-wood, two- and three-story buildings occupied by retail shops, offices, and residences. A twenty-foot-wide alley separated the library from its neighbor.

"This morning about 3 o'clock the sleeping citizens of Newton were alarmed by a cry of fire," reported the *Newark Evening Courier* on September 22, 1873. "There was no wind, but out in the clear starlight could be seen the flames leaping upward and lapping with their great red tongues the buildings that were doomed to destruction. Half-clad men, women, and children rushed into the streets, some carrying with them what they could, others abandoning all property, even clothing, and thinking only of self-preservation. Yet in the midst of this panic-stricken mass of humanity, above the roaring and crackling of the flames, could be heard the word of command from men whose presence of mind rose equal to the emergency and whose spirit was caught by the women and children. Lines were

quickly formed and by passing buckets the brave band did what they could
to put down the flames."

The fire, which had begun at the rear of George Smith's drugstore, rapidly spread to the adjoining hardware store owned by W. W. Woodward,
an L-shaped building that surrounded Johnson's store on two sides. Fed
by flammable oils and paints, the fire now gained headway both on Spring
and Main Streets. Thanks to the shortsightedness of the town officials,
who had allowed the city's volunteer fire companies to disband in 1867,
Newton's firefighting efforts were initially limited to a bucket brigade
manned by women and children and a rickety gooseneck hand pumper
hastily drawn to the scene by former firemen. Matters were made worse
when it was discovered that an underground cistern filled with much-
needed water was inaccessible. After volunteers spent thirty minutes chopping a hole in the cistern's roof, the opening turned out to be too small
to admit a hose. When pumping eventually started, the old leather hoses
burst under the pressure. The chief of the disbanded department, Charles
Crook, who might have brought some order to the confusion, was out of
town on business.

"The towering flames were visible for miles, so that a throng of visitors began to arrive in town to add to the confusion," reported the *Sussex
Independent.* "It was exhausting work to pump those old hand engines.
Many loyal souls stuck to it until their spines creaked and their eyes
bulged out, while others stood around with their hands in their pockets,
refusing to help."

"As the fire swept along Main street the citizens emptied the buildings
of their contents, so that a very large amount of personal property was res-
cued," added the *Newark Evening Courier.* "The book store of Mrs. Rachel
Cramer was quickly consumed, and the residence and millenary of Mrs.
Cummins and the dental office of Dr. R. A. Sheppard went next, and from
here the fire soon communicated to the residence of Mr. Dennis Cochran.
Separated only by an alley from this was the handsome new Dennis
Library, cherished by the people of Newton as dearly as their household

goods. Above the roaring of the flames, the crackling of the fire, the falling of timbers and the shouts of excited men, was heard a great cry from the multitude that clustered at this point. 'Save the Library.' The women and children hurried with buckets of water to the scene, and by the activity, courage and assistance animated the men—it was a fierce battle, human energy and devotion fighting against angry flames, but at last, with thoroughly drenching roof and walls, and beating down the flaming ruins of the buildings opposite, when the beams of sunrise broke upon the scene, the noble edifice was found to the entirely out of danger."

Wet carpets hung over the eaves of the building, and the twenty-foot-wide alley probably saved the library building, which acted as a fire stop on Main Street. On Spring Street an open marble yard marked the farthest advance of the fire on that side. "About 7 o'clock, the fire having been checked both ways, a general sense of relief was felt, for it seemed certain at one time that a great portion of the business part of the town would be destroyed," said the *Sussex Register.* "During the progress of the fire crowds of excited and anxious men and women lined the streets, and either assisted in the work of saving property and checking the fire, or breathing fervent prayers for the staying of the fire fiend. The park and adjoining streets were almost filled with household goods which had been rescued from the burning buildings, and we regret to say that some scamps were so lost to all sense of decency that many articles were stolen—one thief stealing a family bible, which we hope he will read attentively."

As Woodward's hardware store burned fiercely, Johnson's store on the corner "seemed now to be doomed, and men speedily removed the goods . . . , but a hard-working force who remained on top of the building fought the flames with desperate energy, and the handsome building was saved, with but slight damage." A pail-brigade made a dam in the gutter, catching and reusing what wastewater it could.

At its height, the fire was so intense that trees on both sides of Main Street caught fire. Fearing that the entire central business district would be reduced to ashes, telegrams were sent to Morristown, Hackettstown,

Washington, Phillipsburg, Orange, Newark, and Hoboken requesting aid. Because most telegraph offices along the line were closed for the weekend, only Hoboken's fire department was able to respond. Fire bells began ringing there at 5:00 A.M., and soon a special train with firemen and apparatus started for Newton. Hoboken's Steamer No. 1 reached Newton at 9:00 A.M., several hours after the fire had been contained. After wetting down the ruins, Hoboken's firemen ate a hearty breakfast at the Cochran House and returned home on the noon train, refusing to be paid for their services.

While a canopy of smoke still hovered over the town, Newton's governing body met in emergency session to approve the purchase of a steamer and one thousand feet of reliable hose. Within a month of the fire, two new volunteer fire companies were organized.

Newton's most disastrous blaze destroyed or heavily damaged nine buildings and left behind property damage estimated at $120,000. Although its cause was never established, newspapers intimated it was the work of an arsonist. "The origin of the fire is a mystery," wrote the *New York Times.* "The building in which it started was a rear extension to G. L. Smith's frame two-story house fronting on Main street. In this extension Mr. Smith [a druggist] stored his oils and compounded his medicines. On Sunday night he was in the store, and when he left it at 10 o'clock there was a small coal fire burning in a closed stove. It is not known that any other person had access to the building until the fire was discovered." According to the papers, Smith had been burned out twice before.

Caven Point, Jersey City, Refinery Fire—May 10, 1883

A blinding flash of lightning that struck Caven Point, Jersey City, during a thunderstorm that passed over the metropolitan area in the early hours of May 10, 1883, triggered a fire that destroyed what was then the world's largest oil storage depot. Thousands were jolted from their sleep by the storm's rumbling thunder, spectacular lightning, and pounding rain. During the storm, a home in Alpine and a five-story factory near New York's Bellevue Hospital were also struck by lightning and set on fire. The Jersey City depot fire left six workers dead and caused more than $500,000 in damage.

A local reporter on his way to work was passing the National Storage Company's depot on Caven Point when he saw lightning strike one of the oil storage tanks. "The bolt fell nearly straight from the clouds," wrote the newsman, "and . . . almost instantaneously there came the noise of a terrific explosion, which blended with the awful roar of the thunder, intensifying the initial shock of the natural phenomenon most strangely. Immediately following the glare of the lightning, and springing up from the ground like the rebound of it, came the red glare of the burning oil." Tank No. 5, holding some thirty thousand barrels of oil, was soon burning furiously.

Workers at the National Storage facility and the Eagle Refinery next door, many of them residents of boarding houses and tenements near the works, rushed to the scene of the blaze. Firemen from the Lafayette firehouse a mile away, led by Jersey City's Chief Engineer Henry E. Farrier, joined them within minutes. A company fire engine kept at the depot for such emergencies was soon in action, pouring water on the flames. "It was too late," reported the *New York Herald*, "to prevent the ruin. In fact, it was too late at the very instant of the first explosion. The burning oil was scattered about and was flowing over the ground in uncontrollable streams, kindling every inflammable thing with which they came into contact. Streaming toward the water, the flames quickly fastened upon a portion of the wharf and the seasoned wood and the oil blazed up in fury, surrounding four of the largest tanks in the yard."

Jersey City engines Nos. 8 and 9 and truck company No. 10 joined the Lafayette firemen, playing streams of water on tanks and buildings near the burning storage tank. With the fire spreading uncontrollably, Chief Farrier ordered his men back. "We will take every chance to save the place," he said, "but I will not send my men to certain death when there is no chance of doing any good." Just as the firemen were pulling back, there was a tremendous explosion as four additional tanks caught fire. The concussion was heard for blocks around. Heavy brick walls on which the tanks rested were blown in every direction, and pieces of iron flew in the air, some landing as far as a block away. Burning oil began spreading over the easterly side of the depot.

"It was not known at once that any of the men had remained in danger," wrote the *Herald's* reporter, "but almost immediately some of them rushed out with pallid faces, and trembled with excitement as they told of their narrow escape, and of their fear that others had not been so fortunate—a fear that was soon unhappily justified." A hasty roll call revealed that eight employees of the Eagle Refinery were missing.

"No search could be made at once, for the whole of the easterly part of the yard was a blazing sea of oil," said the *Herald*. "Out over the water for a hundred yards the volatile fluid ran as if seeking food for its fury, and the massive volumes of flame that rolled up to the cloud of smoke above carried with them into nothingness the form of everything they touched. Four more tanks were gone, and nigh a hundred thousand barrels of petroleum were now more kindling material for the rest. Nearest to them was a storehouse in which were 40,000 empty barrels, many of which had already been used to hold oil. The very heat ignited them before the flames had eaten through the brick walls from the outside, and almost like an explosion the fire burst forth from this vast house. Less than a hundred feet away stood a similar storehouse in which were as many more barrels, only these were filled instead of empty, and in a few minutes these were bursting like cannon, each adding its own volume of horror to the already almost inconceivable total."

With all of the depot's buildings and its wooden piers now burning out of control, fire officials decided to turn their hoses on the remaining tanks. If they could be kept from boiling over, they reasoned, further explosions might be prevented. By concentrating on the tanks and ignoring the fires, firemen eventually succeeded in saving fourteen of twenty-five tanks.

"After the storage warehouses blazed up the scene was awful beyond description," said the *Herald*. "It was now daylight, and the blinding glare of the flames was tempered by the rays of the sun. The storm above was now past, but the roaring and hissing and crackling of the burning buildings and [rail] cars and oil were almost thunderous. The heavy black smoke rose in the clear air, but it was impossible any longer to make out even the outlines of the rapidly crumbling forms of the buildings in the yard, every one of which was literally enveloped in flames. The tide was at the flood, and that portion of the yard lying to the south of the railroad track was partially submerged with the tide water. Over this ran the oil, and brooks of the liberated fluid also ran in every direction over the land. And everywhere it ran it blazed up, adding to the volume of flame."

By noon, the worst of the fire was over. As two large tanks continued to burn, firemen and plant workers began their search for the missing men. "Yesterday afternoon the scene on Caven's Point was one of utter devastation. One oil tank was blazing furiously, while from under another, which had fallen in, rolled sheets of bright red flame. From both great inky masses of oily looking smoke soared to a great height and swept away to the northward," reported the *New York Times*. "A choking odor of burned oil permeated the atmosphere and made it difficult to breathe, while the smoke from the woodwork rendered breathing almost impossible. About 3 o'clock the firemen got their apparatus together and wearily started homeward. Long afterward, however, the employees of the place continued to pour streams of water into the hot and smoking ruins. A gang of men . . . were busily engaged in the search for some traces of the lost men. About 3:30 o'clock a number of charred bones were found in the place where the missing men were known to have been at the time of the explosion." No further remains of the six missing men were ever found. Among the dead was James Herbert, assistant superintendent of the Eagle Refinery, who it was presumed was working with the others to establish a water line or draw oil off Tank No. 5 when it exploded.

Almost miraculously, James Herbert Jr., the assistant superintendent's son, and William Breese, his adopted son, found safety on Black Tom Island. Superintendent Herbert had ordered them away from the burning tank, and when it exploded they had run for their lives over the trestle connecting the island to Caven Point. When the trestle burned to the water, they found themselves stranded on the island for two hours until a passing boatman who heard their cries rescued them.

Both the National Storage Company and Eagle Refinery were subsidiaries of the Standard Oil Company, a business founded by John D. Rockefeller and others in 1870. Petroleum storage and lighterage facilities were constructed on Black Tom Island and Caven Point beginning in 1876. By the time of the fire—the third major one at the site—the depot had spread over thirty acres, with twenty-five storage tanks capable of holding between 3,500 and 30,000 barrels of oil and kerosene each. Two large brick structures were used to store empty barrels and barreled oil ready for transshipment, much of it to nearby New York City. A Central Railroad siding carried oil tank cars to the depot. A wharf that jutted out into New York Bay provided docking facilities for a half-dozen barges used to transport barrels of oil and kerosene to customers in the metropolitan area. Caven Point, said one newspaper, contained "all of the paraphernalia of a rich corporation doing a prosperous business."

A reporter for Jersey City's *Evening Journal* who visited the disaster site while the depot still smoldered wrote that it "present[ed] a scene of ruin and desolation scarcely to be described." Every one of the buildings stood in ruins. "The brick walls have great fissures in them, as though some gigantic power had bitten great mouthfuls out of them. . . . Eastward of these buildings and between them and the water are the remains of the destroyed oil tanks. The brick foundation upon which the oil tanks rested [are] broken and burned away in places, the intense heat seeming to have calcined the bricks to powder. Nothing of the tanks remains except piles of rusty and twisted and warped iron. . . . The ground, saturated with oil, burned like a peat bed, the ashes being swept away in whirlwinds as soon

as formed, leaving a vast, blackened, unsightly hollow behind, now partially filled with greasy scum and water." The first tank struck by lightning
had almost disappeared. "The shore front presents a scene of black and
charred ground and wood. Bridges, piers, loading platforms, everything
which obstructed the march of the fierce fire, was destroyed. At low tide,
a little way out in the water, are the blackened ribs of the burned vessels,
adding to the desolate scene. In the yard, warped iron work of cars, wheels,
pipes warped into fantastic shapes sprawl unsightly over the ground, and
the railroad tracks strike black kinks and curves into the air in a manner
not at all consonant with the accepted ideas of straight, solid iron rails.
Tank No. 12 stands a monument to the freaks of the fire fiend. Filled with
oil, blackened and scorched by the fire which raged all around it, it stands
unharmed."

According to company officials, the fire destroyed eleven tanks, every
building on the site, the railhead, wharf, bulkheads, and most of the pier.
The total loss was estimated at $500,000. More than forty thousand barrels
of oil had burned.

News of the fire sent a tremor of excitement through the National and
New-York Petroleum Exchanges, both in New York City. When it was
learned that most of the damage was covered by insurance, the price of oil
stabilized at ninety-three cents a barrel. On the afternoon of the fire, company workmen began clearing away the debris; within a matter of months,
the rebuilt depot was back in business.

The Standard Oil Fire, Bayonne—July 5, 1900

Three miles south of Caven Point lies Constable Hook, a stubby cape
located on the north side of the Kill van Kull's outlet into New York Bay.
Mostly farmland until the Civil War, the Hook was transformed in 1864
when the Central Railroad of New Jersey extended its tracks eastward
across Newark Bay and through Bayonne. After the war, the railroad built
the Port Johnston Coal Docks on the Hook's southern shore. At one time

the world's largest coal port, the Johnston Docks soon had a new neighbor. In 1872, John D. Rockefeller's Standard Oil Company set up the first U.S. facility for processing crude oil on 172 nearby acres. Tidewater, Ocean, Prentice, and other oil companies also built storage facilities and refineries on Constable Hook.

By 1885, Rockefeller's Standard Oil had gained control of some 90 percent of the American oil industry, including most of the refineries on the Hook. An industrial complex unlike any other in the world, Standard Oil's facilities included forty stills, ten condensers, a barrel factory, and sixty storage tanks. Crude oil arrived at the Hook, first by railcar and later by pipeline, where it was boiled in the stills, refined in the condensers, and stored in barrels or tin cans for sale throughout the world. The massive green storage tanks, thirty feet high and ninety feet in diameter, were each capable of holding forty thousand barrels of highly flammable oil and related products. It was, said the *New York Herald*, "a region of fume and vapor," a place "from which inky clouds and banks of white vapor of chemicals are constantly rising." In charge of the oil yard was thirty-eight-year-old Superintendent Utley Wedge, who lived with his wife, Grace, and their two young children in one of the better neighborhoods of Bayonne.

In the 1880s and 1890s, thousands of Hungarian, Czech, and Slovak immigrants flooded into Bayonne, drawn by the many job opportunities offered by the oil and chemical companies. The work was dangerous—scores of workers were crushed by machinery or burned by exploding stills—and the pay was low (about $1 a day), but the men came in droves. By 1900, Bayonne's population stood at nearly thirty-three thousand, an eightfold increase in just thirty years. Many of the "Bohemians," as their neighbors called them, lived in overcrowded wooden tenements along East Twenty-Second Street, a few hundred feet from the refineries and tank yards where they worked, ten hours a day, six days a week. Some two thousand men were employed refining forty thousand barrels of oil each day, making Bayonne New Jersey's third-largest manufacturing city and the largest producer of refined oil in the country.

The Standard Oil works was a tinderbox: its buildings, machinery, piers, and even the ground itself were soaked with oil. Mindful of the danger, the company had its own well-equipped fire department, supplemented by firefighting tugs stationed near all the docks. In early May 1900, the docks and sheds of the New Jersey Storage Company, a Standard Oil subsidiary, caught fire. An oil tank ship lying alongside one of the docks was soon ablaze, and within thirty minutes four docks were burning, the flames shooting high into the air. The entire Bayonne fire department responded, joined by fire tugs from the company's Brooklyn and Long Island City yards. A cordon of tugs stood off the piers, pouring thousands of gallons of water on the fire. On shore, the firemen were repeatedly driven back by the intense heat; on the water, the tugs had to turn their hoses on themselves to keep from bursting into flames. When the fire was at last extinguished, a cargo ship loaded with oil bound for China, three barges, three lighters, and a considerable part of the dock had been destroyed, with the loss estimated at nearly $500,000.

The Fourth of July 1900 marked the beginning of seven straight days of the worst heat wave to strike the New York metropolitan area in twenty-eight years. Daytime temperatures hovered in the high nineties while the humidity topped 92 percent. Drenching cloudbursts from passing thunderstorms brought little or no relief. "There was no escape for the perspiring inhabitants," wrote one newspaper, "not a breath of air stirred in the blistering streets, and it was almost as suffocating in the shade as in the sunshine." On July Fourth, appropriately, a lightning bolt struck the Statue of Liberty, doing no damage. The midweek storms were notably violent, hurling lightning down on buildings in Belleville, Orange, Newark, Morristown, and near Trenton, where a man was killed. People passed out on the streets, workers were sent home early, and those who could, sought relief in the parks or on the waterfront.

On Constable Hook, the hundreds of thousands of barrels of oil, kerosene, naphtha, and paraffin stored in the hulking tanks began to heat up. "In hot weather the oil gives off a light, explosive gas," explained a

Standard Oil official. "So much is this the case that in the roof of each tank valves are placed to release the gas after it attains a certain pressure. The very air and atmosphere in the tank yard are surcharged with this highly inflammable gas, and it needs but a spark to cause an explosion." Fires, he added, "are not new to us. Scarcely a week passes by in which one or more of the huge 40,000-barrel tanks does not take it into its head to burn. . . . You can appreciate the danger if you know that a single match or even a spark of a cigar brought within two feet of one of the tanks would cause an explosion."

On Thursday, July 5, at about thirty minutes after midnight, a thunderstorm passed over Bayonne. "While the storm which descended upon the city and the suburbs was at its height shortly after midnight a flash of lightning illuminated the heavens," reported the *New York Times*, "followed almost the same instant by a thunderbolt which was deafening and alarming in its sharp reverberations. These had not ceased when the people of Bayonne, N.J., were startled by three explosions which shattered windows for blocks around." Witnesses said the lightning bolt struck Lizzie Cummings's Bay View House, a saloon and boarding house on East Twenty-Second Street just fifty yards away from the tank yard, setting it on fire. After crashing through the front of the Bay View House, a ball of fire shot out the back "and ricocheting from the ground, . . . successively struck three oil tanks. . . . With a roar that could be heard a long distance, three columns of flames, fringed with black smoke, shot skyward, transforming the night into day." Possibly following a trail of petroleum vapor drifting between the boarding house and the tanks, the lightning ignited the longest, largest, and most costly fire in nineteenth-century New Jersey history. When it burned out seventy hours later, it had caused an estimated $2.5 million in damages. Miraculously, only fourteen people were injured.

As Lizzie Cummings and her two small children fled the burning saloon in terror, a nearby boarding house owned by Mary Connors ignited, sending the fifty refinery workers who lived there hurrying into the street. The Standard Oil Company's fire whistle began wailing, calling the company's

Figure 4. The Standard Oil fire raged for seventy hours, injured fourteen, caused an estimated $2.5 million in damage, and threatened all of Bayonne with destruction. Courtesy of the Free Public Library and Cultural Center of Bayonne.

employees to their preassigned fire stations. By now nearly everyone in Bayonne knew that this fire, unlike so many previous ones, would not be easily tamed.

"Within five minutes after being struck, forty streams of water were playing against the sides of the tanks," wrote the *Times*. "Meanwhile the engineers at the pumping station pumped the oil from the bottom of the blazing tanks into empty storage tanks. Never before had this method failed, but for three blazing tanks the apparatus was no match. The hot weather of the preceding days had caused the oil to vaporize and the very air about the works was charged with the inflammable gases. The flames gaining headway rose higher and higher, and the blazing oil overflowed. It drove the firemen back and communicated itself to other tanks."

By the time the Bayonne fire department arrived, ten tanks were burning furiously. Many firefighters, including company employees who had fought similar blazes before, were convinced the entire complex would be destroyed. On the south side of East Twenty-Second Street oil tanks were on fire. On the north side, less than two hundred feet away, stood Black Tank Hill with four massive tanks holding one hundred thousand barrels of highly combustible naphtha. The fear was that if the fire crossed the street, the entire southeastern section of Bayonne, home to more than 4,500 people, was likely to burn. Connecting their apparatus to nearby hydrants, the firemen played water on the tops and sides of the tanks, cooling them. So intense was the fire on East Twenty-Second Street that paint on the fire engines began to blister. As the firemen donned their heavy turnout coats to shield their bodies from the heat, the chief sent an urgent call to fire departments in Jersey City and Staten Island for assistance.

The massive tanks "boiled and bubbled," wrote one reporter from the *New York Herald*. "The burning tanks were so close to the great engine house and pumping station that it was impossible to transfer the contents of any of the contiguous tanks. Sheets of flame five hundred feet high shot into the air with deafening explosions as one by one the tanks blew up."

"The flames ran along the ground and heated the sides of the neighboring tanks until they bubbled and seethed with the inflammable gases generated in their interiors," the *Herald*'s reporter continued. "The fire ran down to the shores of the bay and caught the scum of oil which rested on the surface. . . . The red glow brought Staten Islanders from their beds." At one point a mile-long ribbon of burning oil spread over New York Bay, headed toward the Statue of Liberty. Another smaller strip of flame floated into the Kill where Wal Van Buskirk for some inexplicable reason lay sleeping aboard his fishing sloop. Seeing the danger, his brother, Phil, commandeered a rowboat and headed toward the sloop. He reached it in the nick of time, jumped aboard, roused his brother, hoisted anchor, and sailed to safety.

While the firemen drenched the tanks on East Twenty-Second Street with water, Standard Oil employees worked methodically to drain oil from other tanks near the fire zone, even some that were already burning.

Pumped into barges, thousands of gallons of oil were transported to safety. Company Superintendent Wedge, in charge of the firefighting effort from beginning to end, sent instructions to Standard Oil tugs in the harbor to tow the fifty ships moored at the docks out into New York Bay. Other men were ordered to drop log booms in a semicircle around the Hook to contain the burning oil slick. Wedge's greatest concern was the burning oil running over the ground, spreading toward other tanks and nearby buildings. Teams of a hundred employees each dug trenches six feet deep and ten feet wide to channel the oil into container basins, where it could burn itself out safely. Other workers spread lime on the ground to absorb the oil.

Standard Oil employees battled the fire for three days straight, often at the risk of their lives. Tank No. 15, which had caught fire on Thursday, was getting so hot that Wedge feared it would explode at any minute. When the

Figure 5. A gang of Standard Oil workers are shown here working to empty a blazing storage tank containing forty thousand barrels of oil, aware that it could explode at any minute without warning. Courtesy of the Free Public Library and Cultural Center of Bayonne.

top of the tank blew off sending burning oil running over the rim, Wedge called for a volunteer to attach a drainage pipe near the top of the tank. A pipe fitter, his name not recorded in the accounts of the fire, stepped forward. "Flames were trickling down the side of the big receptacle, but nevertheless the pipe fitter placed a ladder against the side of the tank and climbed up to the top rung. With the intense heat blistering his face and hands, and small streaks of flame dropping all about him, he bored a hole in the side of the tank and into this inserted the pipe," said the *Herald*.

Most of the city firemen (all of them volunteers) worked three days without sleep. By the second day of the fire they were already so exhausted from holding the heavy hoses in the face of unrelenting waves of heat and smoke that they rigged up improvised stanchions, pointed the nozzles at the tanks, and retreated to safety.

Forty hours into the fire, twenty-three tanks had been destroyed or were still burning fiercely. A monstrous pall of black smoke hovered over the harbor. "By daylight there appeared above Constable Hook a great column," wrote the *Herald*. "Its base was dull red flame, its shaft was smoke of inky blackness and its capital was leaden hued vapor." William A. Eddy, a pioneer meteorologist who worked for the *New York Herald*, calculated by triangulation that the column of smoke rose three miles into the sky.

Thousands of spectators were drawn to the fire scene, lining East Twenty-Second Street or standing on nearby hills for a better view. The Thomas A. Edison Company sent cameramen to film the blaze, creating what may have been one of the first American newsreels. The curious rode the Staten Island ferry just to view the spectacle of burning oil and billowing black clouds. "From the middle of the harbor the column of smoke that ascended from Bayonne looked as though it extended for miles into the clouds," reported the *Times*. "Its black funnel-shaped mass was wafted out over the water by the wind, until at last it descended upon the Long Island coast. Hundreds of people rode backward and forward between the Battery and Staten Island on ferryboats, thinking to get a good view of the fire that way. As each boat passed under the smoky column that formed an arch across the harbor, the passengers forgot the fire altogether and wondered at the sight above them.

"Through the dark canopy overhead a ball of blood red shone out. From it long rays of light shot through the smoke, until a wheel of fire with many radii shaped itself. As the smoke curled and twisted itself in the breeze, the big wheel seemed to be executing fantastic revolutions, and the glowing sphere in the center grew redder and redder every moment. While their boat was passing under the black archway the passengers watched this fiery ball as if fascinated. But when they suddenly emerged into clear air again their handkerchiefs flew up to brush away involuntary tears. For it was the midday sun upon which they had been looking as through a smoked glass." The fire's smoke cast a gloomy shadow over New York Harbor, reaching as far as Coney Island.

New Yorkers crowded the waterfront for a look at the fire. Those who gathered in some of the taller buildings on the west side of Manhattan enjoyed a spectacular view of the Standard Oil disaster. "The explosion and overflow of a big tank during the fire at Constable Hook last night caused some excitement on the roof garden of Koster & Bial's," the *Times* reported. "The flash was of such magnitude that some persons said they could almost read a newspaper by it. . . . When it came those on the roof garden were anxious to get a better view, and they rose from their seats and rushed toward the edge of the roof, where there is a wire caging. The rush was so precipitous that the wire was broken and two or three persons half slipped through. They would have fallen to the street had they gone a few inches further, but the rush was stopped and they were hauled back."

For three days Bayonne hovered on the edge of disaster. So long as the wind blew to the east, the city seemed safe; when it blew to the west, many panicked, fearing that the close-packed wooden tenements nearby would catch fire. "The inhabitants of Bayonne coughed and gasped and spluttered yesterday," reported the *Herald*, "for the augmented heat and the increase of the strength of the acid fumes made the atmosphere almost intolerable. Some of the families who had been driven by the spread of the

fire from their homes in East Twenty-second street, camped on the meadows all night, under the lee of the smoke. Other families, who feared that
the flames might suddenly spread, had their furniture piled up on wheel-
barrows before the doors of their homes." Others, perhaps more used to
oil fires on the Hook, took events in stride. One newspaperman found a
German grocer whose store was near the imperiled naphtha tank dozing
in his doorway. "I vish peebles wouldn't make so much noise," he said. "I
vant to haf a nap." Asked if he weren't afraid, he replied, "Vat's der use? If
it goes oop, it goes oop. I can't help it."

Among the spectators was John D. Rockefeller. Joined by company officials, he arrived in Bayonne on Friday, at the fire's height, stayed several
hours watching the blaze consume his assets, and left without comment.
No doubt Rockefeller confirmed Wedge's plan to contain the fire to the
tanks, thereby saving the vastly more valuable refinery. Both knew that
water could not extinguish burning oil; the hope was to drain away the
oil as fast as possible, to prevent the tanks from exploding (if possible) by
keeping them cool, and to allow the fire to burn itself out.

The fire burned all through Thursday and into Friday with no letup.
"At 10 o'clock last night another tank No. 8 boiled over, sending a column
of flames fully 500 feet into the air causing a panic among nearly 5,000
persons who were on the sand hills as spectators," reported Jersey City's
Evening Journal. "At 2 o'clock this morning the same tank boiled over once
more and the workmen who during the whole time of the fire have been
handling the hose, were compelled to flee for their lives. All day yesterday the flames rolled upward, surrounded by huge volumes of dense black
smoke. Several new tanks boiled over and added fuel to the flames, which
with each accession, rolled upward with a fierce roar, spreading their red
and glittering tongues out over the city. The heat was intense as far away as
Avenue D at these times, and women in the Centreville section fainted or
became hysterical." In fact, added the newspaper tongue in cheek, "from
the reports received there must have been hundreds of women in the city
passing from one hysterical fit into another all day and last night."

Braving the smoke, heat, and fumes, undeterred by frequent thunderstorms and downpours, thousands of spectators crowded the streets
and vacant lots near the scene of the blazing tanks. "During the daytime,
despite the heat, numerous women and girls were to be seen at the fire.
They rode down on bicycles, in the [trolley] cars, some of them coming
from Greenville and Jersey City, and stood in clusters of bright color on
the hills overlooking the burning oil tanks. Both men and women were
inclined to be rash, approaching too near to the open fire pits, so that
the police found it necessary to institute a strong cordon beyond which
the crowd was not allowed to go. An idea of the popular interest excited
by the fire could be obtained at any time yesterday by a stroll on Twenty-
Second Street. Not only were the sidewalks and streets full of pedestrians
and bicycles, coming and going, but also every car that made the trip to
and fro was literally packed from top to bottom. The passengers not only
stood on the platforms and hung on the sides," wrote the *Evening Journal*,
"but were also perched on the roof."

For the firemen and Standard Oil Company employees fighting the
fire, the work was both hazardous and exhausting; for the bystanders, the
scene was unforgettable. On one occasion a boiling tank blew up, propel-
ling its heavy steel roof 150 feet into the sky before it landed on a freight
car with a resounding crash. Later one of the tanks split, making a loud
hissing noise as a sinuous flame shot high into the air. "Just at 10 o'clock
last night a large tank . . . near Avenue I suddenly boiled over," wrote the
Newark Evening News. "The result was that a majestic column of flame
rose nearly 200 feet into the air, and at that moment a sudden puff of wind
from the south carried this flame directly over the great crowd standing at
the corner watching the blaze. The column of fire bent close down upon
them and seemed to lick the upper stories of the buildings by which the
people were standing. For a moment the heat in the street was unbearable,
and in an instant there was a panic. Men, women, and children fell over
each other in the rush for safety, and many were trampled in the muddy
roadway or tripped others."

A few minutes past ten o'clock on Saturday night, after raging for seventy hours, the fire on Constable Hook burned itself out. Destroyed or heavily damaged were twenty-five oil tanks and much of their contents, the boiler shop, compounding and paraffin buildings, huge piles of barreling staves, tons of soft coal, several thousand feet of railroad trestling and scores of freight cars and oil tank cars owned by the Union Tank Line, Lehigh Valley Railroad, and the Central Railroad. Gone, too, were Lizzie Cummings's saloon and Mary Connors's boarding house. Saved were Standard Oil's refinery, a property itself worth far more than anything else on the Hook, and adjacent chemical plants, piers, barges, docks, and refineries, all valued at from $30 to $35 million. The wind, which blew mostly from west to east; the skill, nerve, and brawn of the workers and firemen; and plain luck all factored into the victory over what the *Evening Journal* called "a foe that knew no mercy, a foe that would have consumed a city had not it been met by the men of intelligence and resource."

"The space of the conflagration has a likeness to all large spaces over which a fierce fire has swept clean," wrote the *Evening Journal* after the fire was out. "In a few instances the remains of huge tanks are left standing, but the iron is in jagged point and is eaten away almost to the earth. Tank No. 13, which stood out so valiantly against the assault of heat and flames for three days, is blistered from top to bottom, causing the observer to wonder how the immense vat, full of oil, survived the heat. A chimney of the paraffin works is left standing. The rest of the building has disappeared. Only the battered remains of a stove and a few partly burned girders are all that is left to mark the site of the Cummings hotel and saloon."

"The ground is black," continued the newspaper, "as if in mourning. As far as the eye can see on either side of Twenty-second Street are the signs of a terrible destruction. In the space where a few days ago were the evidence of system and industry is now only the glowing vacancy and melancholy of chaos."

CHAPTER 2

STEAMBOAT DISASTERS

When Robert Fulton's *Clermont* first cruised the Hudson River in 1807, it marked a new era of rapid transportation. Soon every major American waterway was crowded with steamboats, their towering stacks belching black smoke, their side-mounted paddlewheels churning through the water at a steady 5 miles per hour. Magnificent boats paddling down the Mississippi with pennants gaily streaming in the wind may be the romantic image most Americans have today of the age of steam navigation, but for the average New Jerseyan living in the first half of the nineteenth century, steam meant the rugged wooden ferries that joined New York's Battery to the Hoboken docks or Camden to Philadelphia across the Delaware River.

Early steam-driven ferries were little more than rectangular platforms built on catamaran-type hulls, with a coal-burning steam boiler, paddlewheels located amidships, and a rudder at each end. Prow and stern were identical: Instead of turning the vessel around after it reached its destination, the captain simply reversed the machinery. New York and New Jersey were linked by steam in 1811. Ferry service between Camden and Philadelphia began two years later.

New-Jersey—Camden—March 15, 1856

The ferry New-Jersey, built about the year 1840, was the second of that name to steam between Walnut Street, Philadelphia, and Camden's docks. Owned by the Camden and Philadelphia Steamboat Ferry Company, a New Jersey corporation with ties to the hated Camden and Amboy Railroad, the New-Jersey had been entirely rebuilt during the summer of 1855. The vessel had two decks: The main deck for passengers, freight, and horse-drawn vehicles, and about fourteen feet above it, the upper deck, used exclusively for passengers. The smokestack, which protruded through and rose some four feet above the upper deck, was separated for safety reasons from the surrounding woodwork by a steel casing. An ash pan underneath the furnace was an added fire prevention measure. Besides his other duties, the boat's fireman had to ensure a steady flow of water through the pan. The New-Jersey, which could easily accommodate about one hundred passengers, was manned by a crew of four—a fireman, an engineer, a pilot, and a captain who also doubled as fare collector.

On Saturday evening, March 15, 1856, at half past eight, Captain William S. Corson signaled to his pilot and engineer that the New-Jersey was ready to depart Philadelphia's Walnut Street wharf for its regular nightly run to Camden. More than one hundred passengers were aboard, most of them New Jersey residents. Perhaps a third were women and children, another twenty-five or so were free blacks returning home to Camden after a day's work in the city. As Corson backed the ferry into the Delaware River, he discovered that his usual route was blocked by a heavy flow of ice. Turning northward instead, he steered his vessel on a course between the shore and Smith's Island, intending to head eastward across to the Jersey side just north of the island.

Less than ten minutes into the crossing, Captain Corson heard the dreaded cry of "Fire!" Before backing the boat out into the river, the captain had gone down on deck to change the pins in the rudder in order to reverse the vessel, returning to the pilothouse past the smokestack. He saw no fire nor smelled any smoke then. But now his heart sank as he heard the frantic cries of his passengers and saw the angry red flames visible around the stack. Recognizing the mortal peril in which his wooden vessel now found itself, Corson ordered the pilot, Jack Springer, to steer directly for the safety of the Arch Street wharf, only a few hundred feet to his portside.

William F. Agnew, a Camden resident who worked for a Philadelphia express company, was returning home from business in the city. "When opposite Market street, I observed flames bursting out around the smoke stack, and raised the cry of 'fire,'" Agnew told the *Philadelphia Ledger*. "An unusually large number of passengers were on board, many of them women and children. The fire originated in the fireroom during the absence of the fireman and spread with fearful rapidity. It soon wrapped the entire after part of the boat in flames and drove the passengers forward. The strong ebb tide setting up the river convinced me that it was impossible to run the boat aground upon the northern part of [Smith's] Island, and I was glad to see the pilot head for the Philadelphia shore."

Through the smoke Agnew could see Captain Corson standing in the pilothouse shouting orders to his crew. "I was upon the bow of the boat in the midst of a wild heart-rending scene of terror. A crowd of at least one hundred persons, including twenty or twenty-five ladies, were clustered together in the smallest possible space to avoid the intense heat of the flames—some clinging to the guard[rails], others frantically endeavoring to wrench loose the stanchions which were yet free from the devouring element, while some stood horror stricken, gazing upon the fast approaching flames behind, or the icy current before them. There was nothing on board save a bench or two that could be made available as a float or life-preserver. The flames as the wind drove them about increasing in volume every moment caught the dresses of the women, whose shrieks for assistance were appalling. One young girl, Miss Carman, was the only one [I] recognized, and the last [I] saw of her she was enveloped in fire, and screaming piteously. Not until their clothing was burnt from their persons did the passengers seem willing to seek a chance for safety in the bosom of the [river.] One by one, sometimes five or six at a time, they made the fearful leap from the burning deck."

The pilot was able to guide the ferry to within twenty feet of Philadelphia's Arch Street wharf. But just as the captain made ready a line, the steering apparatus suddenly jammed, the pilothouse collapsed, and the vessel shot off at full power away from land and into the channel. "Some on the upper deck, however, had a chance to leap ashore," Agnew continued, "but others fell short and were crushed by the paddlewheels. Every hope of running into the wharves was now dashed, and I turned to Mr. Muschamp, late a conductor on the Camden and Amboy railroad, and asked him if he could swim. He replied that he could not. I advised him to take a bench which was near him, and jump overboard with me. The engine was still going, and I took care to jump clear of the wheels. . . . I swam about 100 yards when I providentially reached the bow of a clipper ship and was rescued."

Figure 6. The steamboat *New-Jersey* provided regular ferry service between Camden and Philadelphia. More than one hundred passengers and a crew of four were aboard when fire broke out on the evening of March 15, 1856. From *Frank Leslie's Illustrated Newspaper*, March 29, 1856.

Like Agnew, most of the passengers had run to the bow of the *New-Jersey* as soon as the fire broke out, hoping to be among the first to reach the wharves and safety. When the ferry neared the dock, a wild panic ensued, with passengers climbing over one another to reach the wharves, many falling into the ice-clogged waters. After the *New-Jersey* unexpectedly pulled away from the shoreline, those left on board, most of them with their clothes on fire, jumped overboard in despair. Many of those who jumped were fatally injured by the rotating paddlewheels.

Samuel Goverson of Philadelphia was on the ferry with his wife and fourteen-month-old child. When the fire broke out, he became separated from his family and was pushed overboard as the boat neared the wharves. Soon after his rescue he discovered to his horror that his baby had drowned. Mr. and Mrs. Nixon of Camden and their child remained on the deck until their clothes caught fire. Separated in the wild scramble for safety, Mrs. Nixon saw her husband for the last time as he was forced overboard with his coat ablaze.

James Ferguson, a clerk, was standing on the stern. "When the fire broke out I determined to stay where I was as long as I could, and fixed the collar of my overcoat around me. I stayed at the stern until the fire drove me away, when I slipped down and hung on the tiller chains. . . . I hung on until I could sustain myself no longer, when I committed myself to the water, with a prayer that God would permit me to see my wife and children once more." Ferguson swam toward the shore, "but I did not know what shore, I was so bewildered. I swam until I was near the wharf, on which people were standing. I felt as if I was about to sink, when they cried out to me to not give up. This encouraged me. I made a fresh struggle, and succeeded in catching a rope. My strength was almost gone, but I hung on desperately, and was finally landed, some of my finger nails being torn off by my efforts to grasp the rope."

A German, his name unknown, was rescued from the ferry's paddle box, his hair singed and his coat burned. "He had a bag of bread with him," reported the *Ledger*, "which he held on to, and took it home none the worse for the accident." John Fidell and his eighteen-year-old daughter, Josephine, were less fortunate. When it became obvious that the ferry was doomed, Fidell tied a rope to one of the stanchions hoping that should it fall into the river, he and his daughter would have something to hold onto. The pair stayed on the boat until the intense heat forced them to jump; moments later the rope burned through, leaving them adrift in the Delaware. Separated from her father, Josephine was saved only when men in a small boat sent out from a schooner to rescue victims of the disaster saw her body floating under the surface and dove down to bring her up.

Major John Sneviley's experience was common to those who were fortunate to survive the fire. He jumped overboard from the stern, his hands and neck burned by the flames, but unable to swim, he used a large picture frame as a life preserver. Of more benefit was his cloak and shawl, which floated on the surface, holding him up until a young black man who had been hanging onto Sneviley's cloak pulled too hard and loosened the buttons. The major, who was picked up by a rescue boat, feared that "the colored boy was lost, although when in the water [I] cautioned him against pulling [my] cloak too hard." Before jumping overboard, Sneviley threw a package of valuable papers and money onto a cake of ice, a package, he told the newspaper reporter, "he would be glad to hear from."

The burning ferry was visible from both Camden and Philadelphia. "No sooner was the fire seen from the Jersey shore, than vast crowds of citizens, and their families, assembled at the wharves, and intense anxiety, alarm, and excitement prevailed; while the atmosphere was lurid with the bale-fires of death, and vocal with the shrieks of the dying—perishing, too, beyond the reach of rescuing aid of friends. Women were seen wringing their hands, children calling for their fathers and mothers, and parents bewailing the supposed loss of their children." A score or more small boats put out into the frozen Delaware to rescue those floating in the water, or clinging to blocks of ice, chairs, or other debris. People on the Philadelphia wharves threw ropes to passengers near the shore. Despite the cold, two members of a volunteer fire company dove into the river, saving a number of exhausted swimmers. Near midnight, the smoldering wreck of the *New-Jersey* lay beached on Smith's Island; dead bodies, most of them severely burned or crushed by the paddlewheels, still floated in the river.

On Sunday, the crowds lining the wharves on both sides of the Delaware watched anxiously as the steam ferry *John Fitch*, in cooperation with several smaller boats, dragged the water for bodies. Although the heavy flow of ice hampered their efforts, sailors on the *John Fitch* fired a small naval cannon to bring up corpses floating beneath the surface. By Monday, the toll had reached nineteen confirmed dead, and thirty-seven missing and presumed dead.

In early April, a Philadelphia coroner's jury, after an intensive investigation, including an inspection of the *New-Jersey*'s boiler, rendered its verdict. The ferry, said the jury, was "entirely unfit for the transportation of passengers; ... she was inadequately manned, her boiler worn out, leaky, and defective; ... there were no boats, life preservers, floats, spare plank, buckets on deck, or any other means provided for the escape of passengers in case of fire, collision, explosion, or any other emergency." The jury found that the fire, originating in the boiler room, gained an unstoppable headway by the time it was discovered because the fireman was required to perform other duties in another part of the ship instead of tending his boiler full-time. "To run the boat on shore, to save the lives of themselves and the passengers, appears to be the one and only thought of the panic-stricken crew."

The *New-Jersey*'s owners claimed that an 1852 act of Congress that required all steamboat pilots and engineers to be licensed and that mandated detailed inspection of steam vessels in federal waters, as well as the provision of life-saving apparatus, did not apply to ferry operators. The coroner's jury dismissed the defense out of hand, finding that "the dictates of humanity," if not the law, required some minimal effort to guard passengers from calamity. Condemning "the niggardly parsimoniousness" of the ferry company, the jury called it a "bloated Shylock" fattening on the "hard earnings of the laborious poor." The burning of the boat and loss of lives was due to the negligence of the Camden and Philadelphia Steamboat Ferry Company, said the jury, adding that its owners were "accessories to this wholesale slaughter."

The wonder is that some other steamboats never actually exploded or caught fire. Early steam vessels used saltwater in their boilers, resulting in heavy scaling; when not properly cleaned and maintained, the boilers leaked, and the riveted seams often ruptured under pressure. Steamboat wrecks made for exciting front-page newspaper stories. Artists employed by Currier & Ives and other lithographers of the time rushed, pen and pad in hand, to the scene of the major wrecks, providing vivid illustrations for a public fascinated by the disastrous shortcomings of nineteenth-century technology.

Isaac Newton—Fort Lee—December 5, 1863

Robert S. Cushing, a frequent traveler by steamboat who had already survived four explosions, boarded the Isaac Newton at Manhattan's Cortlandt Street dock on December 5, 1863, for the trip to Albany. Built in 1846 at a cost of $200,000, with new boilers installed in 1857, the Isaac Newton had been steaming the Hudson River continually for seventeen years. Advertised as "the largest in the new or old world," the boat was 345 feet long, with paddle wheels 39 feet high—taller than a three-story house. It had a top speed of 20 miles per hour. Complimented "for the beauty of [its] architecture and the magnificence of [its] cabins," the ship was "one of the largest steamers on the river and . . . always a popular boat with the public." The captain, Wiliam H. Peck, a steamboat veteran of thirty-five years, had been the Isaac Newton's skipper since its maiden voyage. Casting off at 6:00 P.M. for yet another routine voyage, the Isaac Newton carried its 130 passengers and cargo valued at $300,000 northward at a steady 12 miles per hour.

When the steamboat was opposite Fort Lee, about an hour into the journey, "a terrific explosion occurred . . . , like that of a cannon, and in an instant steam enveloped the different decks." Many of the passengers were in the lower saloon enjoying supper when the blast occurred, "and the first intimation they received was the showering down of live coals upon them, which had been blown from the furnaces by the explosion into and through the ventilator to the lower cabin. On the heads and hands of some fell the burning coals, and the plates they were eating from were filled with them." The burning coals cascading down the ventilator scattered in all directions: A man lifting a cup of coffee to his mouth was struck and burned on his hand; when a red-hot coal landed in another passenger's cup, he was splattered with coffee. A lady's clothes caught fire. "A general horror was the result," reported one newsman. "The steam had rapidly made its way down, and threatened certain death to all. Two men rushed from their unfinished meals, smashed through the forward windows, and crawling out, clambered to the upper deck. The others bent beneath the hot steam, which did not reach the floor, and crawled to the stairway, making their way up."

John T. Bush, a passenger from Niagara Falls, was in his cabin directly over the engines on the port side when the explosion happened. "The noise was a heavy, rushing sound, somewhat continuous, but not extremely loud," he told the coroner's inquest the next day. "[M]y impression was that it was an explosion which was crushing away something, I judged it to be the boiler. I sprang out of my berth and ran forward to ascertain what was the matter. When I returned I saw smoke or steam issuing from the cracks near my state-room, which rapidly increased in volume. Soon after this, on going down the stairs leading from the state-room hall, I met a gentleman, and asked him if anyone was killed; he said there was, and that he stumbled over one person certainly, and perhaps two [who] came up from below who were terribly scalded."

All of the passengers rapidly gathered on the hurricane deck. "There was great excitement, but the ladies, and indeed all the passengers behaved very creditably. Those who had been scalded made a great deal of noise by their groans, which added much to the terror of the scene." The explosion of the steamer's starboard boiler spewed "an unlimited amount of pent-up steam and boiling water into every exposed portion of the vessel," reported the *New York Herald.* "The furnaces, which were in close proximity to the boiler, were blown into pieces by the tremendous force of the explosion, and the red hot coals and burning wood were in consequence cast about the steamboat, setting fire to it, and thereby adding tenfold to the horror of the situation. The luckless vessel was in a few minutes under the full control of the fiery element."

Because most of the passengers were out of their cabins either at supper or relaxing on the after portion of the ship, casualties were surprisingly light: Eight passengers and five crewmen were scalded or burned but still alive; two firemen, the baggage master, and two young bootblacks were missing, trapped below decks in the burning wreckage. "When the true state of affairs became known to the passengers the excitement and alarm . . . [were] perfectly appalling," reported the *Herald.* "The women huddled together in the cabin, in a state of the most abject fear, and the men . . . exhibited scarcely more firmness than their weaker companions. All the life preservers on board the burning steamer were procured and furnished to the females, in case the last extremity of despair should render necessary an attempt to swim for life. . . . The men furnished themselves with everything that might answer the purposes of a body in the water, such as chairs, stools, etc."

It was a raw and blustery night, which made putting out the fire just about hopeless. "The hissing steam and dense vapors enveloped a portion of the vessel in a cloud, through which it was impossible for the men to penetrate in order to take steps to rescue her from her perilous position. The leaping flame was all that could be seen through the smoke and steam, and the vessel was evidently doomed to sure destruction." Cooler heads restrained a number of passengers who attempted to jump overboard. "Many of the lady passengers made wild efforts to throw themselves into the river."

At the sound of the explosion, Captain Peck, who was in the saloon enjoying a meal with the ladies, ran topside, ordered the male passengers to calm the women, and made immediately for the pilothouse, where he directed the helmsman to steer for the shore. At first, Peck could discover

no flames, just smoke and blinding steam, and he told the panicking passengers that there was no cause for alarm. A fire in the baggage room,
however, soon spread to the main salon, despite the efforts of crewmen
manning the few available hoses. Peck lost no time ordering the passengers
and crew to the after promenade deck.

"The main bulk of the people crowded in anxiety to the stern of the
boat, and wildly implored those on shore to render them assistance," the
Herald's account continued. "On the bow of the *Isaac Newton* were congregated about fifty or sixty of the passengers and crew, who were separated
from those on the stern of the boat by a wall of fire and dense volumes of
steam. The fire commenced to burn rapidly, the flames extending towards
the passengers at each end of the steamer, and the situation was beginning
to be extremely critical when, to the joy of all on board, two towboats were
seen coming alongside to render assistance."

The welcome arrivals were a propeller vessel and a tugboat, both of
which had been only a few hundred yards from the *Isaac Newton* when
its boilers exploded. Several canal boats and a number of rowboats that
put out from the shore also arrived at the scene. All of the surviving
passengers and crew were hastily evacuated from the burning steamer
and transported to Yonkers, four miles upriver. "When the [propeller]
was alongside, the ladies and children were first passed on board," said
the *New York Times*. "Several cowardly men tried to crowd in advance of
them, but were summarily thrust back by the brave spirits who sought
to rescue them."

By eight o'clock, the steamer was a mass of flames. "The scene was magnificent," said the *Times*. "The Palisades were lighted up for miles with
the glare of the Demon, and the shore opposite far illuminated." At about
2:00 A.M., the vessel, now burned to the water's edge, sank in about fifteen feet of water, with nothing visible but the iron framing of one of its
paddlewheels.

At Yonkers the injured were made as comfortable as possible. "The
appearance presented by the sufferers is beyond all description," wrote the

Herald's reporter. "Their heads were swelled to twice their ordinary size, and blistered all over in the most dreadful manner. Their faces, hands, and necks were fearfully scalded, and the flesh was hanging loosely from the body, being peeled off. Generally, their eyes were closed, as if destroyed by the scalding water. Their breathing was labored and most painful to witness. The physicians [attending them at Yonkers] informed our reporter that most of the men had been scalded internally, and were the victims of indescribable agony. The cries of anguish which issued from some of the poor fellows was certainly enough to melt the most hard heart. An insatiable thirst seemed to have possession of them all, while at the same time not even the slightest drink appeared to remain on their stomachs."

All of the severely injured died within a day of the accident. The *Herald* noted, "One poor fellow, an Irishman, while writhing under the terrible agony to which he was subjected by the fearful nature of his injuries, feebly beckoned to one of the attendants . . . , and muttered in incoherent language:—'Telegraph to my wife in Albany that I got scalded; but tell her that I will be home tomorrow.' This language, coming, as it did, from a man who it was expected had not an hour's life in him, brought tears to the eyes of several in the room, and they had to turn away to hide their feelings from the poor sufferer."

The final toll was thirteen dead and five missing, all presumed dead. There were countless injuries. With all of the ship's firemen among the fatalities, the cause of the explosion remained a mystery.

CHAPTER 3

TRAIN WRECKS

American railroads are one of today's safest means of travel. Twenty-five times more people are killed per million miles traveled on the highways than on the rails. But it was not always this way. Stewart Holbrook observes that in the early days of railroading, the newfangled iron horses "regularly fell off their flimsy tracks, tumbled down steep grades, hurtled off bridges . . . and collided with each other head on." By the 1850s, as traffic multiplied and speeds increased from 15 miles per hour to 35 or 50, fatal accidents became a regular occurrence.

Early rail travelers literally took their lives in their hands when they boarded. Most pre–Civil War railways had only one track for trains going in both directions, an arrangement that worked only with strict adherence to careful scheduling. Any human or mechanical failure could, and frequently did, prove fatal. Reports of hand brakes that were slow to engage, frail wooden passenger cars that splintered on impact, and kerosene lamps and potbellied stoves that ignited the wreckage outraged America. John Cunningham's *Railroads in New Jersey* cites some of the reaction in the contemporary press. "Butchers," the newspapers called the railroad owners, accusing them of gross indifference to the riding public. "A Collision! We're Getting Used to Them Now!" screamed a Paterson newspaper's headline in 1852, as the increasing number of railroad disasters escalated into a national scandal.

To New Jersey's Camden and Amboy Railroad went the unenviable dis-
tinction of the first train wreck in American history to kill a passenger.
On November 11, 1833, on the line between Spotswood and Hightstown,
a Camden and Amboy carriage derailed and overturned owing to a broken axle on one of the cars. James C. Stedman, a jeweler from Raleigh,
North Carolina, was so badly injured that he died within hours. Another
twenty-four passengers, among them Commodore Cornelius Vanderbilt,
the future owner of the New York Central, were seriously injured. When
Vanderbilt's car overturned, he was hurled down a thirty-foot embankment. In agony from several broken ribs and a punctured lung, Vanderbilt
was taken to his home in New York, where he hovered between life and
death for a month. Another passenger on the train, former president John
Quincy Adams, was uninjured.

Until 1853, a grand total of about fifty passengers had been killed in
railroad accidents. In that one year, amazingly, 234 passengers were killed
in 138 dreadful collisions, marking the beginning of a long history of
nineteenth-century rail disasters that shocked the nation. In 1890, taking
just one example, 6,335 people were killed and 35,362 injured on American
railroads. Cheap construction of tracks, switches, bridges, and wooden
cars was the major cause. Careless employees contributed to the carnage.

The Secaucus meadows were the scene of two of 1853's record-making
wrecks. On May 9, a Paterson and Hudson River Railroad train filled with
immigrants, which was heading west from Jersey City, crashed head-on
with a New York and Erie eastbound express, killing two brakemen. One
day shy of seven months later the same two trains collided head-on in
Secaucus within a mile of the earlier wreck. The brakeman and one passenger died; twenty-three others were injured. "The noise of the collision
was heard for the distance of a mile," reported the *New-York Daily Times*,
"and the farmers in the vicinity hastened to the scene. The baggage car
(No. 2) of the Express train was jammed through the forward passenger
car, sweeping off all the seats. The passengers in this car had a miraculous
escape. Several of them, however, crawled out with bruised limbs and flesh

wounds." The brakeman, Thomas Featherston, "stood on the passenger car platform, and was crushed among the ruins, and mutilated in the most shocking manner. A physician residing at Bergen Five Corners was sent for to attend the dying and wounded, but, we are informed, he refused to go unless he knew before hand 'who was going to pay him.'" Both Secaucus collisions were blamed on crew negligence.

Burlington—August 29, 1855

The first railroad to link New York City and Philadelphia, the Camden and Amboy received its charter from the New Jersey Legislature in January 1830. Along with the charter went a monopoly on what would soon become the busiest rail corridor in the nation, a concession that made sense when millions in venture capital were needed to build the road. As the years passed, the Camden and Amboy zealously protected its monopoly, corrupting politicians and infuriating a public forced to pay exorbitant fares on the only line linking two of the nation's greatest cities. The

Figure 7. On May 9, 1853, two trains running in different directions on a single track collided head-on in a Secaucus cornfield, killing two people. From the *New York Illustrated News*, May 21, 1853.

company's sixty-two miles of track between Camden and South Amboy remained a single line until the Civil War, a tribute to its owner's frugality. To its legion of enemies, the Camden and Amboy's only redeeming grace may have been an invention by Isaac Dripps, the line's master mechanic. Dripps's cowcatcher shoved wandering cattle and horses off the tracks with commendable Yankee efficiency.

One of the nation's worst pre–Civil War railroad accidents took place on August 29, 1855, a half mile east of Burlington, when Camden and Amboy's Philadelphia-bound train, backing up to avoid a collision with the train headed for New York, smashed into a carriage attempting to cross the tracks, killing twenty-two and injuring seventy-seven. The train out of Philadelphia—six passenger cars, a mail and baggage car, and locomotive—reached Burlington an hour before noon, waited ten minutes for the train coming from New York, and then steamed northward for three miles until an approaching southbound train came into view. Following the rules of the road, the engineer of the northbound (or up-train) train blew his whistle, frantically reversed engines, and backed toward Burlington at 15 miles per hour, followed by several hundred yards by the down-train. Suddenly, a carriage driven by sixty-year-old John F. D. Heinaken, a physician in nearby Columbus, appeared on the tracks. Heinaken, who was nearly deaf, had not heard the train's whistle. "The hind car struck the horses, killing them instantly, and this caused that car to be thrown from the track, while those in front piled up on top of it." Four of the six passenger cars derailed "and three of them were utterly destroyed" in what the *New-York Daily Times* called one of "the most fearful railroad disasters that has ever occurred in this country."

William B. Maclay, a former member of Congress from New York, was on the second car from the rear when he noticed that the train had reversed direction. Getting up from his seat for a better look at what was happening, Maclay "heard a whistle and a reply, and saw that a train was on the track before us. . . . I was fearful that we might run off the track or come in collision with the New York train. . . . I therefore rose and left my seat, and had hardly stepped into the middle of the aisle when the collision occurred. I felt a jar, followed with an instantaneous buzzing and clashing of everything about me. I was thrown into the middle of the car and buried beneath the car, amid fragments of broken timber." Riding in the car where most of the injuries occurred, Maclay said he found himself "jammed underneath, a terribly incumbent weight pressing upon my chest, and my legs and arms so closely pinioned it was an utter impossibility to more either of them. I did not dare to move." The groans of the dying and wounded "were most heartrending," Maclay told a reporter. "I was perfectly conscious of my own position, and in the event of any hurried attempt at rescue I greatly feared the mass above me might be let down with increased and crushing weight. Close by me lay pinioned a fellow sufferer, who gave way to expressions of intensest agony and despair. I did my best to cheer and encourage him. He made no reply but by low moans."

A hosiery merchant from New York City, James E. Ray, was in the third car from the rear. When the trains collided, the fourth car from the rear "passed entirely over the one in which he was, making a leap of about 15 feet, and crushing the one under it." Ray, who escaped with minor injuries, said the appearance of the wreck "was frightful in the extreme. The hind car and the one next to it were dashed into small fragments. Of the car in which I was riding there was nothing left but a few bucks and the trucks." Benjamin Mills of Connecticut said the car he was in "flew into fragments instantly." At impact "those in the rear part of the car rushed forward, and I had just risen to beg them for God's sake to sit still, when, before I knew what had happened, I saw the windows and timbers flying in every direction." A man sitting next to Mills was killed, "the back of his head being completely cut off." Mills said, "the first I knew I found myself going through the bottom of the car, and thought my last hour had come. I fell among the trucks, my face in the sand, and my throat across a bar of iron. My leg was badly contused, and I suffered somewhat from internal injuries."

People from Burlington rushed to the accident site, giving what aid and comfort they could to the dying and injured. New Jersey Governor

Rodman Price and Episcopal Bishop George Doane, both near Burlington at the time of the crash, joined the throng. "The ladies of Burlington,
and of the houses in the immediate vicinity of the accident, rendered the
greatest possible hospitality to the unfortunate sufferers," reported the
New York Times. "The Quaker families and others early repaired to the
scene of the disaster, with bandages, linen cloths, stimulants, etc. Many of
the wounded men lie in the houses near the cross roads, and many others
have been taken into Burlington. The houses of that city have been freely
opened, and the bodies of the dead have been all taken thither."

Within an hour of the accident, nearly every physician in Burlington was at the wreck. Telegraphed appeals to Camden and Bordentown
brought more help. Doctors from Philadelphia joined more than twenty
physicians caring for the injured, some of them beyond help. "The groans
of the wounded in the rooms of the hotel at Burlington are described as
awful," said the *Times.* "One man was so injured and his agony was so
intense that he could not remain quiet, but persisted in throwing himself up and down on the settee, groaning terribly." John F. Gillespie of
Natchez, Mississippi, his left leg and right foot amputated, made out his
will before he died, disposing of an estate said to be valued at $600,000.
Gillespie's will instructed his executor to sue the Camden and Amboy
"to the last cent of my fortune" in the event he or his wife, also terribly
injured, died.

The Camden and Amboy wreck, blamed by the coroner's jury on the
carelessness of Dr. Heinaken and the reckless way the up-train sped backward at a rate three times that permitted by law, had at least one light
moment. An Irishman with two broken arms and severe internal injuries
was in the City Hotel under the care of some Burlington ladies. "As he lay
groaning upon his couch, one of the ladies asked him if he could tell where
he was injured internally." His complaint, he reportedly replied, "must be
about the region of the heart, for it could not be otherwise with so many
bright eyes looking upon him."

Hackensack Meadows—January 15, 1894

Nearly forty years were to pass before people in northern New Jersey experienced a train wreck as horrific as the tragedy at Burlington. The highly profitable Morris and Essex Division of the Delaware, Lackawanna and Western Railroad carried thousands of New York–bound commuters to the Hoboken ferries and back home again for fifty-five years without a fatal accident. One of the last of New Jersey's railroads to adopt a modern signaling system, the company relied instead on the tried and true (and far cheaper) method of the past—"sober and trustworthy employees" who obeyed the rules of the road. That reliance came to an abrupt end on January 15, 1894, when the South Orange Accommodation (a short-line commuter train) rear-ended the Dover Express at a drawbridge in the Hackensack Meadows, killing thirteen and injuring more than fifty. Dense fog, faulty signaling, and human error were to blame.

The express train from Dover stopped at Summit to take on two passengers cars of the Passaic and Delaware Railroad from Basking Ridge and Bernardsville, then proceeded east to Newark's Broad Street station, where additional passengers boarded. Because of the dense fog, the Dover Express, which usually left Newark for Hoboken at 8:08 A.M., pulled out several minutes late. The South Orange Accommodation left South Orange at 8:00 A.M., heading for Newark; it departed the city thirteen fateful minutes before schedule. "So dense was the fog, particularly over the meadows, that the men in the locomotive cab could barely discern objects a short distance ahead," reported the *Newark Evening News.* As a result, George Sticher, engineer of the Dover Express, reduced his speed. Approaching the drawbridge over the Hackensack River, Sticher slowed down to about 5 or 10 miles an hour (the accounts differ). "Suddenly the shrill shrieking of a locomotive coming from the rear was heard, and before the rear brakeman of the Dover train was prepared to leave his post to signal the oncoming train the huge headlight of the latter pierced the deep gloom, and the deep rumbling of the heavy train sounded the doom of many in the forward train."

The South Orange Accommodation, with Engineer David Hoffman at the controls, struck the rear of the Dover Express at about 25 miles per hour, telescoping the rear two cars from Basking Ridge and Bernardsville. "There were cries of alarm, warnings were shouted by the trainmen . . . [and] with the shrieking of whistles and clanging of bells, formed an awful din which a second later was lost in the deafening crash as the locomotive went crashing and tearing into the rear car of the Dover train. The engine plowed through the car, shattering iron supports and making splinters of massive wooden beams. Several cars were telescoped and the locomotive of the train that caused the disaster was stripped of its pilot, the headlight was torn off and the heavy iron work was twisted like so much putty." Engineer Hoffman jumped from his locomotive at the last minute, cutting his legs and head as he landed on the embankment. His fireman, Irving Metz, ran to the rear of the engine, climbed over the tender and jumped seconds before the crash.

"The scene that follows beggars description, " wrote the *News*. "Men and women sprang from the platforms and went tumbling down the embankment in their efforts to escape. The terrified shouts of hundreds who fought and struggled in their wild frenzy to free themselves from the mass of unfortunates, some dead, others wounded in a dozen different ways, mingled with the heartrending cries of the sufferers, and lent an additional horror to the catastrophe." Shouts that the wreckage was on fire added to the bedlam. Passengers who jumped to avoid the supposed flames were injured needlessly before it was discovered that escaping steam, not smoke, was the culprit. Trainmen and volunteers hurried to extinguish the coals in the stoves of the smashed cars to prevent fire.

"The scene on the foggy meadow will never be forgotten by those who witnessed it," reported the *News*. "Trainmen and stalwart passengers heaved and hacked with axes and saws at timbers that wedged in sufferers and dead. Women fainted, and even men turned away from the mangled

Figure 8. This woodcut depicts the last car of the Dover Express impaled on the engine of the South Orange Accommodation. From the *Newark Daily Advertiser*, January 15, 1894.

and distorted forms that were borne one by one from the two smashed Summit cars. The headless body of Edward T. Morrell was taken out and laid on the embankment and the head was not found for some minutes afterward, and then under a seat six feet in front of where he sat."

The rear car of the Dover train, a combination smoker and baggage car, remained on the tracks, its roof and sides so badly damaged that they threatened to topple over at any moment. The two cars in front of it had derailed.

Edward W. Gray of West Summit, a twenty-three-year-old passenger in the car ahead of the Dover Express smoking car, told the *New York Herald* that he was looking out the window when he heard one of the train hands shout through the door in the rear, "Jump for your lives!" "Then there was a terrific crash and I knew no more," recalled Gray, who suffered a compound fracture of the left leg and lacerated hand. "I awoke, I know not how long afterward, with timber piled on top of me and all around me. I felt no pain at first, and remember saying to myself—'Well, I suppose I'm going to kingdom come.' The next thing I made out was smoke, and I immediately thought that the car was on fire and that I should be burned alive. Then I raised my eyes and saw Sanford Tyler, a boy I knew, climbing through the roof of the car. I could just see his legs. . . . I called to him and he shouted back. 'Don't be scared. I'll fish you out!' The boy was as good as his word, and after what seemed an age he and a couple of men returned through the roof and pulled me out the same way."

Seventeen-year-old Tyler, on his way from Summit to his job with a New York newspaper, was one of several Good Samaritans who helped with the rescue work. Sent flying through the roof of his car by the impact, Tyler rolled down the embankment but except for a gash in his scalp was unharmed. Grabbing an axe, he set to work breaking open the roofs of several cars and with the help of bystanders extricated passengers trapped by the smashed wooden timbers and collapsed seats.

Rosa Archer, a primary school teacher at New York's Vesey Street School, had spent the weekend with friends in Summit. "The first intimation I had of anything wrong was a tremendous crash," recalled Miss Archer, who was sitting near the stove in the next to last car of the Dover Express, "and instantly the lighted lamps were extinguished and the steam was shut off. In the same second everyone in the car screamed. Then another crash came and I was violently thrown forward and looking up saw the sky. Then I realized that I was lying on my back and that timbers were falling over me. I tried to move but found myself pinioned fast. The weight of the smashed car timbers were added to by the stove, but fortunately they fell so as not to crush me. Shivered glass flew through the air, and I felt a warm stream gently trickling down the right side of my throat." Everything happened within a matter of seconds, Archer, cut on her head and neck, told the *Herald*'s reporter, "and in the next I saw men and women struggling to free themselves. I cried for help again and again and almost immediately was answered. A passenger heard me and called railroad hands. Then they pried the timbers which pinioned me, and throwing a cloth over my face to hide the horrid sight . . . they lifted me upon a stretcher and carried me into an empty car."

Washington Irving, grandnephew of the famous author, was sitting in the smoking car when the crash occurred. "Just ahead of me, and on the same side, were four gentlemen whom I know very well, who were engaged in a game of whist. I was watching the game at intervals, and occasionally one of them would address a remark to me. . . . The crash came while I was talking. It seemed to me in that dreadful moment as if I saw in one brief flash the card players, their board and the seats they occupied swept away as though raised by a cyclone. I recovered my senses in time, but the pain was awful. I was buried under splintered wood and could not move. I was finally pulled out by the boy Sanford Tyler and a man I do not know." Despite a serious spinal injury, Irving was one of the lucky ones: three of the four whist players were among the dead. According to the *New York Times*, when Irving recovered consciousness, he found one dead man lying across his legs and another, who was dying, clinging to his neck.

"Suddenly we felt a great jolt, followed by a crushing sound, and the train came to a sudden stop," W. W. Shouler told a *Newark Evening News* reporter. " I got out and ran ahead and the sight amazed me. . . . The cars and locomotive were in a confused mass. On the track lay a man apparently about 60 years of age badly cut and bleeding. He was either dead or unconscious. Three or four mutilated bodies strewn about and on the tracks lay in pools of blood. I looked down the bank and there lay a body that was horribly torn and mangled. Another man was calling faintly for whisky. I looked inside one car and saw another man creeping along the floor with one arm torn off."

G. F. Gifford of Newark was sitting in the car in front of the smoker when the crash occurred. "I scrambled out of the train and went to work getting out the other poor fellows," he told reporters from the *Evening News*. "One of the first men I saw was Mr. Rolliffe, a clerk in the Garfield National Bank. He was in a frightful condition. There was a hole in his chest from which the blood was pouring, and his head was a mass of wounds. He recognized me and managed to undo his watch and chain. Then he asked me to take his diamond studs out of his shirt. He asked me to take them to his wife with his last message. He was still alive when they took him to the hospital." A few minutes later Gifford found an unopened bottle of applejack whiskey along the track. "I started through the forward car with it and gave it out to the injured."

"Before I could rise from my seat after the first sound of the crash, I saw the sides and top of the car being doubled up, the ragged ends of the broken timber thrust into some of the passengers' bodies or knocking them down," explained Robert G. Hann Jr. of Summit to the *Evening News*. "If something had not stopped it, one heavy piece would have hit me in the face with terrible force. I saw another man just dodge a beam by sliding from his seat to the floor and the timber passed where his head had been."

Most of the injured were in the last three cars of the Dover train. Some of those sitting in the cars behind the South Orange engine were also injured, but less seriously. Thomas Fenner, a New York cotton merchant, was sitting only four rows back from the front of the first car. Reading a newspaper when the crash happened, he was thrown to his feet by the impact. "Instinctively he ran toward the rear of the car. It happened that no one obstructed him, for the car carried not more than a dozen passengers, who got out with all possible haste. As Mr. Fenner ran," said the *Times*, "the car lamps fell, and the car was filled with glass flying from the windows. He had not reached the rear door when he felt the floor bulging beneath him, and when he jumped from the platform the sides of the car caved in." New York Produce Exchange member W. T. Wells was in the third car behind the local's engine. So great was the force of the collision that had he not clutched the seat ahead of him, he said, he would have been tossed forward two rows. "So much strength was required to hold himself back that he wrenched his arms and neck. As he plunged forward he saw a man hurled from the front platform of his car to the opposite track, from which he rolled over the embankment," reported the *Times*.

Men working at a nearby slaughterhouse heard the crash, groped their way through the dense fog and were among the first rescuers at the scene. Two fishermen who hurried from their shanties on the Hackensack River to the collision site described the carnage to the *Newark Evening News*: The last car of the Dover train and the engine of the Accommodation were driven together, they said, with the engine under the platform of the express. The trucks of the Dover car were off the tracks, one side of it had been ripped off and the seats, partitions and everything in it "crushed into a heap of ruin." The cars ahead of the last Dover car were partly off the tracks, their windows were smashed and their platforms crushed. "Two men lay dead in pools of blood, near by dozens of injured men and women were running about dazed, crying and wringing their hands, and the crews of both trains were busy getting the dead and dying out of the wreck."

Louis Bodine, a student at New York's College of Physicians and Surgeons, happened to be on the Accommodation. Although badly cut on the forehead and his right hand "horribly mashed," Bodine treated the injured as best he could. "I want to have you record the heroic services done to the injured by Dr. Louis Bodine," Washington Irving told the *Herald*'s reporter. "He was badly cut about the head and face, but he went about, the blood streaming from his wounds, rendering what aid he could to those who were worse off than he." After working at the accident scene for an hour, Bodine was bandaged up and made his way home to Summit. A passenger on the Accommodation, the Reverend Wallace of Seton Hall, chancellor of the Newark Archdiocese, gave last rites to some of the dying.

Another hero of the wreck was Warwicke Greene, a fourteen-year-old on his way to school in New York. After the crash, he joined the crew and other passengers in an impromptu rescue team, aiding the injured, dousing the stove embers, and chopping away wooden beams that entangled wounded passengers. "He threw his overcoat over his head and groped under an engine from which scalding water flowed like a brook," said the *Times*. "He lifted mangled bodies that had breath, extricated them from entangled masses, called for aid when loads were heavy, remonstrated with his admirable will when faintness threatened." According to the newspaper, he "worked incessantly for two hours . . . , covered with mud and blood, like the hero of an epic poem."

One of the first physicians at the wreck site was Dr. Joseph B. Bissell of New York, a passenger on a train behind the Accommodation. "The fog was very thick," Bissell told the *Herald*'s reporter, "but we were running along at what appeared to be the usual speed when suddenly the train came to an abrupt halt, and on looking out I saw a number of trainmen running back and learned that something had happened ahead. A minute or two later a brakeman came through the train looking for a doctor, and I went up the track with him to the scene of the wreck. I shall never forget that sight.

"The rear car of the first train had been simply demolished, and its place on the track was occupied by the engine of the second train, which appeared to have sustained little injury. Wounded people were lying on both sides of the track, and I could hear the frantic cries of those who were imprisoned in the wreck of the forward cars. Dead men were scattered here and there like logs of wood, and I counted nine corpses when I reached the spot. The trainmen were already busying themselves in extricating the wounded and removing them to the forward cars, which had escaped injury.

"The conductor of the express was particularly active in this work, although he seemed himself to be badly injured about the head. In the third car from the rear I saw many persons who had their clothing torn off, but who seemed to have escaped with trifling injuries. I found it impossible to attend to the wants of all that were hurt. While I was attending to one I was surrounded by others, who frantically besought me to bind up their hurts. How many people I attended to I cannot say, but I finally selected five of the most seriously injured men and with the aid of the train hands had them laid on improvised beds in the forward car of the wrecked train. All of them had broken limbs and numerous cuts and contusions, in addition in some cases internal injuries." After an hour, Bissell and his patients started off for Hoboken. On the way, two of the five died of their injuries. A rescue train from Newark with four physicians aboard had reached the site at 9:30 A.M. after groping through the fog and confusion.

News of the accident quickly reached the Newark and Hoboken stations. From Newark a large crowd of concerned relatives and sightseers began the seven-mile walk to the accident site, meeting along the way a throng of uninjured passengers from the two trains involved in the collision and several from Newark that stopped behind the wreck. According to the *Newark Daily Advertiser*, relic hunters "were busily engaged in tearing off pieces of the wood work of the wrecked cars which lay at the foot of the embankment" until the police intervened. Scattered along the tracks and down the embankment were the personal belongings and clothing of hundreds of passengers, parts of the engine, splintered wood and stuffing from the seats. "Mixed in the debris, and lining the tracks for 50 yards, were thousands of roses, shipped from Madison and Summit for the New York market. These were eagerly picked up by a crowd of relic-hunters, who even picked them from pools of blood and thrust them into their buttonholes."

At Hoboken a crowd of some five thousand gathered at the terminus and ferry station, anxious for news. When the first five cars of the Dover Express arrived with the dead and injured, the police had all they could do to keep the surging crowd away from the platform gates. The dead, all horribly mangled and one decapitated, were placed in a railroad shed. The walking wounded were cared for in the YMCA rooms, then taken to Saint Mary's and the Presbyterian hospital. Some of those who walked off the train carried their arms in slings. Others wore bandages on their heads.

"All [of the injured] were soiled with earth or car dirt, and few had whole garments," reported the *Times*. "One or two declined to go to a hospital, and waited until they could procure conveyance home. Of those who could walk, the majority hurried out of the station without troubling to give their names, and either crossed to New York or went to hotels or barbers to make themselves presentable." Two who walked nonchalantly to the Duke House near the station "washed their faces and hands, took a drink, and went away." All of the dead were from Millburn, Summit, New Providence, Basking Ridge, and Bernardsville.

Newsmen at the scene blamed the Accommodation's engineer, David Hoffman, for the wreck. The *Times* focused its wrath on Hoffman's supposed carelessness, insisting that "signals had nothing to do with the accident." S. T. Bray, secretary to the railroad's general superintendent, admitted that warning flags on the rear of the express might not have been positioned correctly. "If, however, the flag was properly displayed and Engineer Hoffman failed to slow up, the blame for the accident would rest on him." The fireman on the South Orange train, Irving Metz, defended Hoffman: "We were going about 25 miles per hour, and suddenly there loomed up in front of us the Dover express. . . . The fog was so thick that we got within 100 feet of the train ahead before we saw it at all. . . . I don't know who's to blame, but I do know that there were no signals for us to stop. The signals read all right."

Samuel Sloan, president of the railroad, blamed Engineer Hoffman as well, telling the *New York Times* that Hoffman "was running at too great a speed, considering the weather conditions, and he was too close behind the Dover train." Although he conceded that Hoffman, a twenty-year veteran of the railroad, had performed splendidly just a year earlier when his train accidentally derailed at the Orange station, Sloan maintained that the Meadows accident "was not due to defective signaling but to a violation of the rules laid down expressly for the guidance of trainmen in just such cases. . . . We have a system of safeguards that is sufficient, if men can be depended upon to obey the rules made for them."

The signal system used by the Morris and Essex Division consisted of torpedoes and flags during the day and torpedoes and red lanterns at night. Whether the railroad's system of signals was adequate would be debated in the newspapers for days after the accident and by a coroner's jury that convened in Hoboken in late January. On February 9, the jury found that the primary cause of the accident was the failure of the Dover train's flagman to signal the train behind it that the express had slowed. The secondary cause, said the jury, was that the Delaware, Lackawanna and Western "has no proper signal system between Newark and the Hackensack bridge for the prevention of accidents." Engineer Hoffman was exonerated.

The railroad promptly accepted responsibility for the wreck, settling all claims for death and injury out of court. Within a month of the accident, the time-honored system of torpedoes and flags was replaced with automatic block signals, a proven safety feature that nearly all major railroads in the East had installed years earlier.

May's Landing—August 11, 1880

Atlantic City is a creature of the railroad. Before 1854, Absecon Island was a forlorn place, home to seven families who eked out a meager living from the sea. Flat and sandy with a ten-mile stretch of magnificent beachfront, the island was virtually uninhabited except for countless mosquitoes, black snakes, and greenhead flies that lay in wait for the unwary visitor. It was the beach that intrigued a local politician and visionary, Dr. Jonathan Pitney, who for two decades dreamed of transforming the lonely stretch of sand and surf into a "bathing village" or health resort where fresh air and sparkling salt water would cure everything from rheumatism to insanity.

A railroad link between Philadelphia and Absecon was the key to development. With capital raised in Philadelphia, Pitney and his business associates built wharves and a station at Camden and sixty miles of single track across the Pine Barrens, opening the Camden and Atlantic Railroad on July 1, 1854. Christened Atlantic City, the tourist village that soon rose from the dunes was billed as a place of "rest and relaxation" for Philadelphia's masses. And the masses responded, slowly at first and then after the Civil War in unimagined numbers. By 1870, more than three hundred thousand excursionists rode the Camden and Atlantic to Atlantic City, mostly on day trips. Two additional lines, the Philadelphia and Atlantic City Railway, which opened in 1877, and the West Jersey and Atlantic, inaugurated in

June 1880, competed for the Philadelphia trade. By the summer of 1880, when the weather held, the three roads brought an astonishing twenty thousand passengers to the resort each weekend. The trip from the Camden wharves to the Atlantic City station took less than ninety minutes.

Backed by the Pennsylvania Railroad, the single-track West Jersey and Atlantic was well built and competently managed by the standards of the day. Calculated to attract "the medium and poorer classes," the West Jersey and Atlantic charged fifty cents for a round-trip excursion fare (compared to $1.75 on the other roads), even less if a group charter were arranged. On the evening of Wednesday, August 11, 1880, two sections of a West Jersey excursion train left Atlantic City for Camden carrying nearly 1,300 men, women, and children home to Philadelphia's Saint Ann's Roman Catholic Church after a day at the beach. It was raining heavily as the two sections left the Atlantic City station, the first at 6:00 P.M., the second five minutes later. At May's Landing, some seventeen miles from the resort city, the first section pulled off the single track onto a siding to allow the passage of the 5:30 P.M. express from Camden to Atlantic City. A moment after fourteen of the sixteen cars of the first section had turned onto the siding over the Great Egg Harbor River, the train's second section of eight cars suddenly came into view.

In an instant the second section collided with the last cars of the first section, tearing the rear car open, killing twenty-six passengers and injuring at least fifty-five. A dense cloud of high-pressure steam and jets of hot water escaping from the engine's ruptured cylinder heads scalded many of the dead and injured. Initial telegraph dispatches from the accident scene reported two or three dead and a score injured, although badly. The true dimension of the catastrophe was revealed only the following day, when newspaper reporters reached the scene.

According to witnesses, a handful of excursionists standing on the rear platform of the first section were the first to realize the danger, some jumping from the train and others rushing panic-stricken back into the car. "The locomotive then came bounding on and crashed into the rear car, still standing upon the switch," reported the New York and Philadelphia papers. "So terrible was the force of the collision that the engine fairly ploughed a furrow half way into the car, the roof of the latter being lifted over the smoke-stack of the locomotive. The shock broke one of the cylinders of the engine, and instantly scalding water was poured out upon the terror-stricken occupants of the car. The rain had been pouring down heavily, and consequently all of the windows of the car were down, and the steam filling it instantly added to the terrors of the occasion by concealing everything under an impenetrable cloud. . . . The panic-stricken thousands in the cars of the first train ran pell-mell from them or jumped through the windows and rushed they knew not wither in their unconquerable fright."

The president of Saint Ann's Literary Institute, T. B. Judge, was in the rear car of the second train when the crashed occurred. "The shock was a strong one, and several persons were thrown from their seats," said Judge. "There was the appearance of a panic, and I did all in my power to quiet it. I partly succeeded and then the people began to leave the car to see what was the matter. I went with the rest. When I reached the head of the train I saw a sight which I cannot adequately describe. The injured passengers were being drawn from the car, and the water on each side of the track was filled with persons who had jumped from the train and were up to their waists in the river. A boat soon put out and picked them up. On the embankment of the railroad, which is about seven feet high, were the sufferers from the crushed car, groaning in their agony."

Although painfully scalded on the face, hands, and feet, iron merchant Thomas J. McGrath was able to give a graphic account of the disaster to a *New York Herald* reporter. "I was sitting about four seats from the end in the last car—the car that was telescoped. I saw the engine that wrecked us coming up behind at lightning speed. Our brakeman had just stepped out to place the danger signal (a red lantern) on the rail, or he was about to do it—I don't know which—when the crash came. Now I am an old railroad man, and I feel almost positive that the engineer of the approaching train did not 'shut off' up to the time of the accident. Why do I think so? Because the cylinders of the engine burst, and the steam having free vent poured out in torrents with the scalding water into the car. Had the throttle valve been closed it could not have escaped.

"As soon as I felt the shock I ran a few yards up the aisle and dropped between two seats," continued McGrath, who later died from his injuries. "The broken timber and ironwork were piled on top of me, and I could feel the steam prickling my arms and legs, which were exposed, like a thousand red hot needles. Although my sufferings were intense I struggled to get loose, but without avail, and if some one had not freed me I believe I would have died right there. The shrieks and groans of the poor women and children were something terrible, for you know a scald or burn does not stun a person like if they had been wounded by a piece of flying timber, but it only makes them appreciate the agony more keenly." McGrath railed against the engineer of the second section. "I truly believe that the engineer must have been drunk or crazy. The road was an open, straight one, and it was daylight. Why, God bless me! Couldn't he see the other section coming, and know that a smash up was unavoidable? Four or five jumped off and into a ditch and saved themselves. Why couldn't the engineer see us, as well as we could see him, and stop his train in time to avoid a collision? Indeed," continued McGrath, as a spasm of pain passed over his face, "if the wretch had been caught I wouldn't have given a farthing rushlight for his life. They were after the wretch with clubs and pistols, and I can tell you hot Irish blood wouldn't have stood on much ceremony with such wicked carelessness."

"I was sitting by the window about the middle of the last car of the first section, and happened to look back, when I saw the second section close behind and coming at what appeared to be full speed," John Kelleher told the *Philadelphia Inquirer*. "I was too far from the door to get out in time, and jumped from the window, landing in the mud and water beside the road. I was the first one who left the train. The car was full of people, and as far as I have ascertained I am the only one of them who escaped uninjured. The scene was an awful one, I can assure you; and a great deal of indignation was expressed against the engineer of the second section, who would certainly have been lynched by the people had he not jumped from the engine and made his escape."

Mary Kramer, who was on the third car from the rear of the first section, said she felt "the shock, and knew that an accident had occurred. I went back among the injured as soon as I could get out of the car. Nearly the first one I saw was poor Mary Henratty, who was fearfully burned. She said, 'O, mother of God, what will become of my poor mother.'" Frederick A. Shower, standing on the rear platform of the last car of the first section, "noticed the train coming to a halt, and on going to the rear door to ascertain the cause I saw the second section coming down on us rapidly. I gave the alarm and started for the front of the car, but had not reached it [when] the engine came crashing through the door I had just left. Immediately the car was filled with a dense volume of hot steam." Shower jumped from the car into the river.

A Camden newsboy was on the second section hawking the evening papers when the crash occurred. "Just as I entered one of the cars I was thrown violently on my back," said Robert Lee. "As soon as I could get off I ran to the front end of the train where the people were rushing from the cars through the windows and doors."

Seated in the third seat from the rear of the last car next to William Fallon, Kate Taggart was among the lucky ones. As soon as Fallon saw the approaching train, he pushed Miss Taggart out a window then jumped after her. Taggart was badly bruised on her face and body as she rolled down the embankment. Fallon ended up in the marsh. There were other miraculous escapes. According to the *Newark Daily Advertiser*, "a little girl 18 months old was in its mother's arms when the collision occurred and the father, snatching it quickly without waiting to raise the car window threw it through the glass and jumped after it. The baby was afterwards picked up only slightly injured."

A *New York Times* reporter interviewed "a lady from Philadelphia" who had been in the third car from the front of the last train: "I heard three crashes, one after another, and then came a volume of smoke, which blinded me so that I could not see anything," she told the reporter. "I was close to the door and jumped off as soon as I could. I saw the people all smashed up. Some were so scalded that the flesh was hanging from their faces, and they were in the greatest agony. Others who were cut up or had their bones broken were crying for help." People from May's Landing brought flour, oil, and bandages, she added, doing what they could to help the injured. "Some of the people that I saw were badly burned on the arms and hands," continued the lady. "The flesh on one woman's hands was hanging in shreds. I saw one little girl jump out of a window. Several people fell into the creek from the cars, and one young lady was only saved from drowning by the greatest of exertions."

Survivors of the crash (among them Father Quinn, a parish priest) were quick to blame Edwin T. Aiken, the engineer of the second section, and his conductor, Charles Hoagland. Despite the heavy rain, they claimed, Aiken had an unobstructed view of the first section and should have been able to stop in time. "It will undoubtedly go hard with Aiken, for Father Quinn, the excursionists and the authorities of the road all seem to hold him accountable," said the *New York Herald*. As the *Herald* reporter was walking from the station back to the wreck, he met two men "very much frightened and hurrying along." Questioning them, he discovered that one was Engineer Aiken, who claimed "there was a crowd of the roughest characters on the train looking for him, saying they would lynch him as soon as they could lay their hands upon him or shoot him on sight." The *Herald* correspondent hurried back with the men to the May's Landing depot, helping them open a baggage car where the frightened pair hid themselves for the night. "The feelings against the engineer of No. 3 were so strong that even Father Quinn entered into it and said that hanging would not be too good for him," wrote the *Herald*'s reporter. "A young man on the down train, wearing a long white linen duster, was somehow recognized as a clerk in the Camden office of the road, and in the dark some one cried out, 'Shoot the *** in the linen duster, or make him tell us where the engineer is!' This was enough warning for the young man; so he took off his wrap and was lost sight of in the crowd which surged in front of the depot in the pouring rain." The depot itself was chaotic. "All over the floor and benches of the waiting room lay the injured, screaming and moaning alternately, while without peal after peal of thunder and a furious gale did not tend to make the situation any more cheerful."

"The excitement [in Atlantic City] is intense, and an attempt was made to mob the railroad employees," added the *Herald*. "A freight clerk was assaulted with a pistol, but he knocked his assailant down and ran. The other railroad men were compelled to change their clothing." Conductor Hoagland, who kept his uniform on despite the danger, later called the excursionists "a pretty rough crowd."

One of the heroes of the wreck was Special Officer Leon Hartley, hired by Saint Ann's for the Atlantic City excursion. He saved three lives. "When the scalding steam was pouring into the car three men in their agonized frenzy leaped into the river, and Hartley, who had escaped unhurt, jumped in after them. After protracted struggle he succeeded in getting them all out and into an undamaged car." Dr. Edward T. Reichert of Philadelphia, the only physician on the train, was eventually joined by four local doctors from May's Landing and nearby towns. The injured were taken to Colonel Baker's Union Hotel and several private houses in May's Landing, then a tiny village clustered around three churches, Baker's hotel, and a cotton factory. Volunteers applied a mixture of flour and water to the scalding victims. Little could be done for passengers who had inhaled the steam, which seared their lungs.

News of the accident was telegraphed to Camden and soon spread to Philadelphia. Thousands gathered at the wharf to await the victims. "[T]he excitement of those looking for their friends at the wharf, as the wounded were brought over from Camden, was intense," reported the *Times*. "Some of the women had gone down to the seaside in light Summer costume, which furnished but light protection against the steam-jets, and the only difficulty is to see where they are not burned. They were carried from the cars on reaching Philadelphia a mass of flour and cotton, under which the human form was scarcely distinguishable, and but for the low moans, they seemed dead."

After Aiken emerged from his hiding place the morning after the accident, he and Hoagland were arrested on a charge of manslaughter. Held on $1,000 bail each, the engineer and conductor testified at four separate inquests in May's Landing, Camden, and Philadelphia. Engineer Aiken insisted that he was running about a mile and a half behind the first section at only 25 miles per hour when he rounded a curve and spied the first section on the side track. Aiken swore he applied the air brakes, and when they did not work, pulled back on the throttle and opened the sand boxes for added traction. As the train slid along the wet rails, Aiken gave four signals on his whistle "to let the first section know that I was coming." It was a close call, said Aiken, an eighteen-year veteran of the railroad who had been an engineer for a year and a half. "If I had had another car's length I could have stopped the train in time to have prevented the accident."

Other inquest witnesses contradicted Aiken, including two Atlantic City police officers who said the two sections left the city's station not more than a minute apart, which was a violation of railroad rules, and by a company foreman who testified that when he examined both the engine and the cars, none of the wheels showed evidence of any flat surfaces, proof, he said, that the train had not slid any distance.

The Philadelphia inquest was the most thorough, stretching over four days. After examining the collision site at May's Landing and the wreckage in Jersey City, the jury reached its verdict on August 23, finding that the accident might have been prevented if Aiken "had more carefully observed the rules and regulations of the company," or in other words, either the engineer didn't know the right way to work the air brakes or he had been following the first section too closely or both. The Camden jury, which interviewed twenty-eight witnesses, reached similar conclusions but also blamed wet rails and "some unforeseen cause to this jury unknown."

Absecon Island—July 30, 1896

It was 6:30 on the evening of Thursday, July 30, 1896, when some 250 exhausted members of the Improved Order of Red Men boarded their special excursion train at Atlantic City's railroad depot for the return trip to Bridgeton. The day had been delightful: the resort's famed boardwalk, crowded with amusement rides and vaudeville shows, taffy parlors and beer gardens, offered entertainment for the whole family. Stalls where Kewpie dolls and racy postcards were sold and Gypsy fortunetellers who gladly parted the visitor from his cash filled the numberless arcades. The beach sparkled in the hot sun, the surf welcomed those daring enough to shed their inhibitions. For Bridgeton's Red Men and their families, the train ride home would be a time to relax, pour the sand out of their shoes, and relive the excitement of the day.

Three railroad lines connected Atlantic City with the mainland and points north and west. The West Jersey and Atlantic Railroad and the Camden and Atlantic, both controlled by the Pennsylvania Railroad, and the Philadelphia and Reading Railroad all ran out of the resort on approximately parallel tracks. After crossing a drawbridge, the West Jersey line swung to the left where, about two miles west of Atlantic City, it approached the double tracks of the Reading at an obtuse angle. A wooden signal tower manned by an operator marked the spot just below the Thoroughfare (the channel separating Absecon Island from the mainland) where the West Jersey tracks crossed the Reading at grade level. A semaphore directed traffic at the crossing during the daylight hours. After sundown, a red light ordered approaching trains to come to a complete stop; a white light signaled safety. It was an extremely perilous arrangement, to be sure, but one that a skilled engineer could take in stride, confident that any train approaching the busy crossing would instantly obey the operator's signals.

Engineer Edward W. Farr of Camden, a cautious, experienced railroad man, was at the throttle of the Reading Express as it thundered eastward at 45 miles per hour. A few hundred yards away the West Jersey excursion, John Greiner at the controls, headed westerly toward the intersection. Although Farr and Greiner saw each other as they both neared the intersection, Greiner, who had the white light, kept his hand firmly on the throttle, certain the express would stop. The West Jersey locomotive had just cleared the crossing when the powerful Reading engine smashed into the car behind the West Jersey locomotive at an oblique, crumpling and overturning that car and the car behind it as well. Propelled by the force of the collision, the Reading engine and the first car of the express and the first two cars of the excursion train scraped along the marshy right-of-way, plowing into a water-filled ditch. The third and fourth cars of the West Jersey train telescoped into each other but remained upright on the tracks. Minutes after the collision, the Reading locomotive's boiler exploded, scalding some to death and throwing boiling hot water over the injured lying nearby. "Many of the excursionists who had been thrown from their train were crushed beneath the Reading locomotive, or were slowly scalded by escaping steam," reported the New York Times. "Many of the excursionists saw the approach of the express, and, knowing there would be a collision, tried to jump from the cars. But few were successful, however, and when the collision did occur, were buried beneath the wreckage. The third car of the excursion was crushed to pieces. In that car most of the people were killed. The car turned over and in a few minutes it was set on fire. . . . Those who were not killed instantly but remained trapped beneath the wreck saw the blaze about them and cried out piteously either to be killed or rescued."

On board the express out of Philadelphia, Julius Price sat in the smoker behind the baggage car. He told the Times, "As we came to the tower. . . . the train came to a halt with a severe jolt. The shock was so pronounced that it swayed us all forward, then back, and then forward again. None of us in the smoker was hurt; I doubt whether any were even bruised. Several of us hastened to the forward car of those overturned. By the time we reached it those of the passengers whom the collision had left able to free themselves were scrambling out of the windows. We helped as many as needed it, and then made our way into the car. Half a dozen people were lying about inside amid the wreckage of seats. It was here that we fully realized the horror of the accident. The first woman we took out had her leg cut off between the knee and the ankle. A man we took out afterward evidently had his back broken. We got out as many as we could, but the cars were so smashed that it was impossible to remove all by the doors. We set to work digging away portions of the shattered roof of the second car and carried out a number through the opening."

Price was appalled by the carnage. "I saw at least 25 persons lying apparently dead on the bank, whither they had been removed. There were many others pinned in the debris who could not be freed without the aid of mechanical appliances. With one of the passengers in my car I helped carry a man who was internally injured to a spot where a number of others lay who had been hurt. On the way he told us in broken words that he feared his entire family was destroyed—his wife, his child, and his wife's father and mother. As we lowered him to the ground, a woman all bandaged came up panting and sank beside the sufferer, crying: 'Harry, Harry! O my God! he's dying.' At another place were a mother and child together. The mother, hurt internally, was unable to move. The child, also injured, clung to her torn dress and cried to her for aid; but the poor woman could not speak, much less raise a hand to aid. These sights were everywhere, and the injuries of some of the victims were too ghastly to describe—sightless, battered faces on breathing bodies, crushed and mangled forms with eyes upturned in pain and the lips moaning inarticulate anguish."

Some narrowly escaped death. The *New York Times* reported that Charles Blue of Bridgeton, seated in the rear car of the excursion train, found himself completely turned around after the impact, but uninjured. Two children who sat directly in front of him were crushed to death. In the middle of the same car a family of four sat facing one another. Seeing that a collision was inevitable, the father threw his young child as far out the window as he could. "The child alighted on a soft bank and sat there

Figure 9. Wreckage from the crash of the Reading Express and an excursion
train carrying 250 members of the Improved Order of Red Men lies scattered
along the tracks in this photo taken the day after the 1896 collision. Courtesy
of the Atlantic City Free Public Library.

cooing while the rest of the family were ground to death. Another man was
passing from the first to the second car when he saw the oncoming train.
Without hesitation he sprang off the platform, sustaining no more serious
injuries than a sprain."

Moments after the accident, the signal tower operator telegraphed the
news to Atlantic City. The city's firemen rushed to the crossing, doing
heroic service through the night and into the next morning. The *Times*
report continues, "All the people pinned under the cars were not dead, the
cries coming from them being plainly heard. A huge bonfire was started,
and this was kept burning nearly all the night. Among the first of the bodies to be taken out were those of a man and a woman. One of the man's
hands clasped that of the woman, and his other hand was stretched rigidly

out in front of her, as though at the moment of death he had thrown it out in a vain effort to protect her. Both faces bore the stamp of fright and agony. The bodies were carried to the grass and put down, still clasped together in the embrace of death. A whole family was found—mother, father, grandmother, and child. All were dead save the child, who had escaped injury. When found the terrified child was clinging to the crushed breast of the dead mother. It fought when it was taken away. . . . One of the most awful sights was when a party of rescuers found a human heart impaled on a splintered portion of a car." Alongside the tracks the Atlantic City firemen found little pails and shovels, a nursing bottle, a baby's rattle, torn and bloodied clothing, and a man's leg.

As word of the wreck spread across Atlantic City, thousands of curiosity-seekers joined firemen at the scene of the accident. They came by bicycle, carriage, or omnibus or simply stumbled along the tracks in the dark. Most came to gawk. A few helped the firemen as they worked to rescue the injured and recover the dead.

"The scene at the wreck can not be described," the *Newark Evening News* reported. "The groans of the wounded mingled with the hysterical screams of those seeking relatives and friends among the dead and injured. As each mutilated body was taken from the wreck it was surrounded by a crowd of anxious ones seeking to identify it." A gray dawn was just breaking in the east when rescuers came upon Engineer Farr's body, pinned under the Reading engine. After hydraulic jacks raised the locomotive, ten volunteers dragged the body out. Force had to be used to release Farr's grip on the air brake and throttle. Beneath the engine's tender the firemen found the crushed remains of a young girl. Nearby was the body of Charles McGear, stuck headfirst in a pond.

Special trains brought the dead and wounded back to Atlantic City. At the Reading Railroad's excursion house rows of bodies were laid out in black boxes. Identification of the remains proceeded slowly amid scenes of terrible grief. The Newark paper told of one man from Bridgeton who entered the temporary morgue. A policeman opened one box. It was the man's father,

Figure 10. The flimsy construction of many of the wooden passenger cars in use on American railways during the nineteenth century is evident in this photo. Fifty died and at least another sixty were seriously injured near Absecon Island. Courtesy of the Atlantic City Free Public Library.

"mangled and twisted." The box next to it was opened. In it lay the dismembered body of the man's sister. During the morning a fireman delivered "a ghastly bag" to the morgue containing seventeen feet, all but one clad in russet shoes, the distinctive footgear of the Red Men. The feet ranged in size from the silk-clad foot of a toddler to those of full-grown men.

The wounded were treated at city hospitals or in hotels after the hospitals filled to capacity. In the morning a special train from Philadelphia brought fifteen surgeons who joined nearly every Atlantic City physician in helping the thirty most seriously injured survivors.

More than five thousand people gathered at the West Jersey station in Bridgeton as a special train from Atlantic City arrived bearing the bodies of the dead. "The crowd stretched out from the depot in every direction for hundreds of feet and gloomily awaited the train," said the *Evening News*. "When it rolled up to the station the scene was of an intensely sorrowful nature. Sobs and cries of anguish could be heard on every side. Women wrung their hands and sobbed convulsively and strong men cried like children." In Atlantic City, the boardwalk was deserted, the amusement booths and pavilions shuttered "and the presence of death could be felt everywhere." Bandaged survivors walked the streets from one temporary hospital to another, searching for relatives. Too often, their quest ended among the forty-four bodies laid out in the morgue. A final count put the number of dead at fifty and the seriously injured at more than sixty.

A final casualty was the wife of Reading engineer Edward Farr, who had been found with one hand on the throttle and the other on the brake. When told of her husband's death, she fell to the floor dead of a stroke.

A coroner's inquest a week after the accident pointed the finger of blame for the collision squarely at Engineer Farr. All the witnesses agreed that the express had the red signal, the excursion train the white. Why Farr ignored the danger signal until it was too late was never determined, although the evidence proved that at the last minute he had applied his brakes. In an interview with reporters, Atlantic City Mayor Franklin Stoy waxed philosophic. Sad and terrible though the accident was, said Mayor Stoy, it would not interfere with the resort city's prosperity. "Such accidents occur but once in a number of years," he assured the reporters, "and it is almost certain that no such horror will ever cast its gloom upon the city again."

Bordentown—February 21, 1901

Franklin Stoy was still mayor of Atlantic City five years later when the resort suffered another horrendous train wreck. Again, human blunder played its usual role when a wreck near Bordentown claimed seventeen lives and terribly mutilated another forty-six would-be Atlantic City visitors. Blame fell squarely on a careless conductor who disobeyed his orders.

The Pennsylvania Railroad's crack New York–to–Atlantic City express, the Nellie Bly, named for the celebrated woman journalist who had circled the globe in record time, contained three sections on February 21, 1901, to accommodate the large crowds heading for a long Washington's Birthday weekend at the Jersey Shore. Each section was supposed to travel several miles behind the other. The third section, engineer Walter Earle at the controls, left Jersey City at 3:14 P.M. packed with excursionists from New York, Connecticut, and Rhode Island. About thirty Italian laborers employed by the railroad sat in a combination baggage car and smoker directly behind the locomotive. Stopping at Trenton, the Nellie Bly picked up some pottery workers and a convivial group of delegates who had just attended a Knights of Pythias convention.

Fifteen minutes after the express train pulled out of Jersey City, the Bordentown Accommodation, a local passenger train that ran between Camden and Trenton on the Amboy Division of the Pennsylvania, started north from Camden for Burlington. At Kinkora, B. F. Thompson guided the local onto a siding to allow the Nellie Bly's first section to pass. Steaming toward Bordentown, Thompson's train stopped at the station, chugged north a few hundred yards, then pulled onto another siding as the express's second section sped south on the single line of track. "As a general rule we pass the third section at Rusling's Station," said Thompson later to the *Newark Evening News*, "but we received no orders that another section was due and we put on full steam and made for [Trenton's] Clinton Street Station."

It was now 5:30 in the evening. The Accommodation had just rounded a curve two and a half miles north of Bordentown when Thompson spied the fateful glare of the Nellie Bly's headlight directly ahead. It was the third section. "My God, here comes a train!" shouted Mike McGowan, a fireman on the Nellie Bly. "Jump and save yourself!" the engineer, Walter Earle, bellowed. "Hurry! Hurry! Hurry!" McGowan jumped and landed in the grass, suffering a deep scalp wound but escaping with his life. Earle stayed at his post, blowing the whistle and applying the brakes for all he was worth.

"The express had made frequent stops on the run down from New York," a passenger told a reporter from the *New York Times*, "and was slowing up just north of Bordentown when the accident occurred. At this point there is a curve. The first thing the passengers knew was a sudden jolting of the train caused probably by the engineer putting on the brakes, and the next moment a terrible crash. Both engines were reduced to a mass of broken and twisted iron. The car containing the Italians was crushed to splinters, and all its occupants were buried under the mass of wreckage. The second car piled up on the first car, and the third car crashed into the mass and tumbled into the canal alongside the railroad." Engineer Thompson jumped into the dry canal bed moments before the crash, breaking both legs and an arm and suffering internal injuries. Earle hugged his controls to the last, the impact throwing him against the fender of the northbound train and decapitating him. His head was later found twenty feet from his body. "When the awful crash came passengers were thrown in heaps, the two engines were reduced to scrap, four cars were almost completely demolished and the wreckage caught fire," reported the *Newark Evening News*. The Nellie Bly's smoking car, baggage car, and a Pullman sleeping car derailed, rolling down the embankment and sliding into the canal.

"It was on the Nellie Bly express, in the forward coach between the engine and the baggage car that the greatest number of fatalities occurred," wrote a *Trenton Evening Times* reporter from the scene. "There, crowded on the seats, were about 30 Italians, on their way from New York to begin construction work in Atlantic City. Few of these came out alive. The frail coach was crushed like an eggshell when the engine and baggage car closed in on it, and a moment later blazed up . . . when the stoves overturned. Behind the baggage car was a day coach crowded with excursionists on their way to spend Washington's Birthday at Atlantic City. This car was overturned as if it were a feather and thrown into the canal, which runs on both sides of the high embankment. Behind the Nellie Bly baggage car, which was not badly damaged, lay an overturned passenger coach, which was riven and literally torn to shreds. These cars were thrown to the right

Figure 11. Hundreds gathered on the banks of the Delaware and Raritan Canal near Bordentown to gawk at the twisted remains of the Nellie Bly. Courtesy of the Trentoniana Collection, Trenton Free Public Library.

of the track by the terrible force of the collision. One stood upright in the canal bed and the other lay overturned on the bank."

The death toll would have been much higher had the Delaware and Raritan Canal been full of water. Scores of passengers ejected through the broken windows into the canal bed would have drowned; fortunately, because it was winter, there was only a trickle of water in the canal. "The most terrifying feature of the wreck," said the *Newark Evening News*, "was the fire that broke out immediately from the shock of the trains. The stoves were overturned and then, while the passengers in the rear coaches looked on helpless and miles from aid of any kind, the wretches pinioned down beneath the burning cars were roasted to death."

When the crash came, conductor Edward Sapp of the Accommodation, who had been standing, was nearly thrown from one end of the car to the other. His head badly cut, he wandered amid the wreckage. A short time later, John Thaler, a Trenton pottery worker walking home, met up with Sapp, "half staggering and with a wild haggard look on his face, going toward Bordentown." Sapp was on his way to summon help.

Passengers were crushed between the colliding cars or thrown out of the windows, then killed when the tumbling cars landed on top of them. The *Evening News* reported that Mrs. Harry Lyons and Mrs. Belle Freedman, both of New York City, sat talking together in the third car of the Nellie Bly when the force of the impact threw Mrs. Freedman off her seat, ripped the seat from its fastenings and propelled both the seat cushion and Mrs. Lyons through the window. As she flew out the window, Mrs. Lyons caught the sill with one hand just as her long hair tangled in the sash. Hanging by her hair, she dangled in mid-air, her feet unable to touch ground until the car settled further into the canal. Gaining a precious foothold, she hung precariously from the side of the car until a fellow passenger cut her hair and carried her to safety. George Enger of South Orange, an invalid, was sitting in his wheelchair in the baggage car when the trains collided head-on. The baggage car splintered, part of it landing on top of the car in front of it. Miraculously, although Enger was thrown out of his chair, he was unhurt. Crawling to an opening in the wreckage, he was saved by a fellow passenger searching the ruins for the living or the dead.

Survivors of the wreck pitched in to save their fellow passengers. "Windows were hastily broken and the wounded who could be reached were lifted from the ruins. Many were pinioned between the seats and their cries and groans were heartrending." As the rescue began, said the *Evening News*, "ghouls made their appearance at the wreck. Small parties of boys and men flitted about in the shadows of the wrecked cars, seeking valuables in the ruins." Pictures, brass decorative pieces, pocketbooks, and other articles lost by some of the victims were carried off into the darkness. There were no doctors or nurses on either train, forcing the passengers to fend for themselves. "When the crash occurred calls were made for physicians but it was not until one of the conductors [probably Sapp] volunteered to walk to Bordentown, a mile and a half in the snow, that any effort was made to secure proper medical assistance."

Two hours passed before any doctors arrived. In the meantime, a second-year student at the University of Pennsylvania Medical School who happened to be on one of the trains "worked away on 20 injured passengers. This youth, with a big jack-knife sawed off three legs and bandaged ten others. He likewise instructed the train crews and male passengers on first aid to the injured and an impromptu medical corps . . . was set to work." The coach the Italians were riding in caught fire, "and in the falling darkness the flames shot up like beacons, signaling in the night around for aid to the distressed." Baggage master James Birmingham was among those pinned in the wreckage. As the approaching flames drove off rescuers trying to free his legs, Birmingham repeatedly called for help. When a bucket brigade eventually managed to put out the fire, the baggage master was already dead. Most of the injured trapped in the wreckage who could not be reached died when the fire engulfed them. Thomas Lawrence of Trenton told an *Evening News* reporter that he saw one man buried beneath the ruins, his shrieks and moans piercing the cold winter air. Try as he might, Lawrence could not free the man in time.

A story printed in the *Trenton Times* five days after the accident sent chills down the spines of the survivors who read it. According to the paper, "a package of a particular aspect was taken from the ruins and when it was examined later in Camden . . . it was found to contain dynamite." The only explanation was that some of the Atlantic City–bound laborers planned to use it on their construction project. "They would have use for the stuff in their work and it is thought some of them were carrying it as baggage to save expense and to avoid the difficulty attending the shipment of explosives. It is said there is nothing unusual about these men carrying dynamite in this way and it seems to be the only reasonable explanation." The coroner reported that the package contained fifteen pounds of dynamite, enough to blow up several passenger cars.

Figure 12. The force of the impact between the Nellie Bly and the Bordentown Accommodation sent wrecked engines and coaches into the nearby
canal, killing at least seventeen. Courtesy of the Trentoniana Collection,
Trenton Free Public Library.

The surviving members of both train crews were perversely uncoop-
erative. They refused to run a car with the injured back to Trenton, claiming that they would be disobeying orders if they did and might lose their
jobs. After members of the Bordentown fire department who battled their
way through the heavy snow began playing water on the burning coaches,
the crew ordered them to stop, saying they preferred to let the debris burn.
Worse, surviving passengers charged that wreckers sent to the crash scene
by the railway company neglected to search the smashed cars thoroughly,
ending their work even though three badly injured Italians still lay trapped
in the tangled wood and steel.

About half the dead were Italians, most from New York's Lower East
Side. The youngest fatality, Giuseppe Maida, was fifteen. The only female
casualty was an unidentified woman believed to be Italian. Rescuers had
been able to pull her upper body from a smashed car as flames scorched
her legs. But her arm wrenched from its socket and she fell back into the
wreckage. Efforts to identify her one-armed corpse were unsuccessful.

The dead were carried by train to Trenton, the wounded to Trenton, Camden, Philadelphia, and Atlantic City. "Never before were there such scenes at Clinton Street Station, Trenton, as when the first train came in bearing the dead and wounded," said the *Evening News.* "The cries of the wounded . . . could be heard at the ticket office upstairs. Hundreds congregated to see the wounded brought upstairs, and, while they shuddered at the awful sight, they seemed bound to the spot by an awful fascination. . . . There were a dozen physicians on hand. But little could be done for the sufferers in their condition and surroundings, and they were sent at once to St. Francis Hospital. The seats of the cars had been torn apart and made into cots. The men lay on these, suffering the most horrible agonies, and the picture was most appalling. Down the cheeks of some streamed tears. Even beneath the smoke and blood on the faces of others could be seen the pale shadow of death."

Initially, the cause of the disaster was blamed on a mix-up of orders. Before he died, engineer Thompson claimed that his instructions were to wait for the second section of the Nellie Bly to pass before reentering the main track. "If the orders directed my train also to wait for the third section," said Thompson, "the figure three must have been small and indistinct." Edward Sapp, the conductor of the Accommodation, himself badly injured, was guarded in his comments to the press, acknowledging only that when the second section of the express passed his train, it signaled that a third followed behind it.

At a coroner's hearing held in Trenton the month after the accident, Sapp ruefully admitted that the wreck was probably his fault. His thumb, he told the coroner, just might have covered up the part of his orders that told him to wait on the siding until a third section of the Nellie Bly had passed. Sapp was charged with manslaughter, arrested, and held on bail. In June, the Mercer County Grand Jury decided not to indict him, instead handing up a stinging presentment that censured the Pennsylvania Railroad for running both north and southbound trains on a single track that lacked the "latest devices calculated to protect the life and limb of travelers."

Although seventeen were officially pronounced dead, the actual number may have been higher. "The death list will never be fully known," editorialized the *Trenton Times*, "as the hungry flames . . . may have consumed many whose absence may never be accounted for." Today, New Jersey Transit's River Line runs along the same tracks the Nellie Bly traveled, still carrying commuters between Trenton and Camden.

The Thoroughfare Wreck—October 28, 1906

On October 28, 1906, a three-car train of the West Jersey Seashore Electric Railroad, motorman Walter Scott at the controls, was making its regular Sunday afternoon run across the meadows from Pleasantville to Atlantic City with one hundred passengers aboard. Approaching the Thoroughfare, scene of the 1896 wreck, the West Jersey tracks climbed a twenty-foot-high wooden trestle, then crossed the swift-running tidal stream on a mechanical drawbridge described by the *New York Times* as "of the latest improved type." To bridge-tender Daniel Stewart, a twenty-five-year veteran of the railway company, and his assistant, Thomas Russo, went the job of raising the drawbridge for ocean-going vessels. Once a ship cleared the bridge, Stewart and Russo were required to inspect the locking pins to be sure they had slipped back into place, then signal a nearby tower operator who swung a lever, securing the pins and simultaneously setting a semaphore one hundred yards from the bridge at "all right ahead." The bridge mechanism was designed so that if the pins securing the rails were not aligned precisely, the tower levers operating the semaphore signal could not be moved.

Motorman Scott, who normally would have been relieved at Millville, swapped trains instead with another motorman in order to spend Sunday evening with his wife in Atlantic City. No doubt Scott saw the fishing schooner *Sinbad* pass under the drawbridge as his train rushed across the meadows and onto the trestle at 20 miles per hour. Whatever thoughts Scott may have had of the evening ahead were his last: As the train rolled onto the bridge, all three cars derailed and plunged into the murky waters of the Thoroughfare. Only the third car, its rear wheels caught on the embankment, remained partially above water. "Caught in the first and second cars, locked in by lever-moved doors which they could not open, the helpless pleasure seekers were drowned," a reporter on the scene from the *Newark Evening News* wrote later. "The cars sank quickly, and in a few moments the last of the entrapped victims had yielded up the struggle. A few persons escaped from the forward cars by breaking the windows and crawling out, to float to the surface, where they were picked up, bleeding and unconscious." At least sixty-five people drowned almost instantly, among them motorman Scott. "To one fact is attributed the escape of as many as did get out. This was the failure of the third car to go completely off the drawbridge. . . . Those in the rear of this car had a chance to make their way out and to assist others who were thrown to the forward end of the car and found themselves in the water, which rose rapidly in the coach."

Most of the survivors of the wreck smashed their way to safety through the windows or crawled up the aisle of the third car to the embankment. Mrs. McDonald of Philadelphia, a passenger in the second car and "expert swimmer," broke the window next to her, rose to the surface for air, then dove down to rescue her husband and three other men. The force of the impact threw another Philadelphian, Henry Deemer, against a window, breaking the glass. He managed to free his wife and reached the surface only slightly injured. In the second car, as it plunged under the water, David Emley realized that his only chance was to get a window open and float to the surface. Lifting eight-year-old Helen Gilbert, a friend's daughter, to an open ventilator for air, he fought his way to a window, smashed it, returned for Helen, made his way back to the window and swam to the surface. Emley told reporters that as he made his way from the ventilator to the window, he stumbled over his fellow passengers on the floor of the car. They pulled at his feet and tried frantically to cling to his legs, said Emley, but he shook them off as he made his way to safety.

The conductor, James Curtis, felt that something was amiss as the cars reached the bridge, turned to investigate, felt a "peculiar sensation" and the next moment found himself under water. "I can't remember just exactly what happened," said Curtis. "All I can think of now is that when I found I could not escape any other way I broke through the window with my fists. I had an awful time getting out, because a colored man seemed to be struggling the same way. I managed to get him through safely, and then I swam away and here I am." William H. Stewart, who lost his wife and child in the wreck, owed his survival to a bell rope. "Just before the drawbridge was reached," explained Stewart, "I got up to put on my overcoat. In reaching for one of the sleeves my other hand went up in the air and touched the bell rope. At the same instant the car went off the track, and in a second all was darkness. I grasped again, caught the rope and followed it to the rear of the car."

Rescue efforts were well under way within minutes of the disaster. Andrew K. Brady and his friend, John Quinn, in Atlantic City for a Knights of Columbus outing, were standing near the Pennsylvania Railroad terminal talking to an acquaintance when they heard the fire alarms sound. "We immediately hurried to the scene of the wreck and reached the place not more than 20 minutes after the accident occurred. I was a railroad man once and have been in wrecks and have seen others, but this one was the worst I have ever witnessed. When we reached the scene frantic efforts were being made to rescue the imprisoned people from the two submerged cars and the one that was partly under water, but was suspended by its rear end from the abutment of the draw. The work of rescue was pitifully impotent, however, because of lack of means and facilities to get at the interiors of the cars. The water at that point was about 20 feet deep at the time and the tide was rising. The cars are of steel and formed death traps to those confined inside them."

Even after it became certain that no one could be alive in the submerged cars, police and firemen struggled bravely to reach the bodies. Brady talked briefly with a man named Lawrence, who said he had been in the first car. "He was utterly unable to account for the manner of his escape, nor could he tell anything about the disaster and what had been the effect upon the people in the car with him of the first shock of the plunge into the water," Brady told the press. "He was hardly accountable, poor fellow, for what he was saying, as he had had his child with him and the little one was among the dead. We saw a number of bodies taken from the submerged cars. Men worked as best they could with oyster tongs and boat hooks and every once in a while they succeeded in bringing a body to the surface. Most of these were women and children and each succeeding find added to the heartrending nature of the accident."

Most of the dead or injured were from Philadelphia, including eleven members of Tosca's Royal Artillery Band. Entire families drowned, making the task of identification difficult. The dead lay in an improvised morgue, and at ten o'clock Monday morning a crowd of "wretched and suffering ones seeking lost ones were permitted to enter the chamber of death," said the *Newark Evening News*. "Most heartrending were the scenes, and men who had worked with strong arms and hearts to bring out the bodies from beneath the waters of the Thoroughfare were moved to tears. Among the most pathetic cases was that of Samuel McElroy of Philadelphia, who after a sleepless night found his family wiped out by the disaster, his wife and five-year-old daughter lying dead in the morgue and his three-year-old boy Joseph missing. When the officials making record of the identification asked for his address, the broken-hearted man replied: 'It was 2029 Green street, but I shall never return there—God only knows where I shall go.'"

As an investigation into the cause of the Thoroughfare wreck began, railroad officials claimed that a flaw or crack in one of the passenger train's wheels might be to blame. When cranes lifted the derailed cars from the water and set them on the rails, however, no defect could be found. "After a thorough investigation," the officials admitted, "we have found no explanation of the accident. . . . All possible theories were traced to the bottom,

Figure 13. Efforts to retrieve the submerged passengers cars of the Thoroughfare wreck were delayed when one of the rescue engines overturned after it plunged through the trestle. From a postcard.

but the cause of the derailment of the electric train is no better known than it was at first." A coroner's jury viewing the bridge looked hard at an outside rail of the southbound track that was torn from the ties and twisted at a point where it joined the drawbridge tracks. They concluded that the drawbridge mechanism had failed to align the tracks exactly, causing the cars to derail as they rolled over the skewed rails. Reporters who visited the accident site were amazed at the flimsy trestle construction and the lack of guardrails on a structure elevated twenty to forty feet above ground level. "Even after electric cars began to run there were reports that expert engineers had condemned the Thoroughfare structure . . . ," revealed the *Evening News.* "These experts said that the contractors, in their hurry to get the bridge done and the line opened, had sacrificed durability to save time. Constructed of light timbers, the settling of which is believed by the county authorities to have thrown the draw mechanism out of plumb, and made it necessary to sometimes close the rail link by hand, the bridge, even to a layman, looms from the banks, as the experts said, unsafe for even a trolley car."

There were other theories, too. Some said that Stewart, the elderly bridge tender, had gotten into a violent argument with the crew of the *Sinbad* as it passed under the draw. He was so infuriated, went the rumor, that he scarcely glanced at the track alignment before signaling all clear to the tower. Why the so-called safety mechanism failed to work was never explained.

CHAPTER 4

SHIPWRECKS

More people died in maritime disasters along the Jersey Shore than from all other nineteenth-century catastrophes combined. "The coast of New Jersey is more famous for shipwrecks, attended with loss of life, than any other part of our country. The wonder is," said a state official in 1848, quoted in Francis Lee's history of New Jersey, "not that so many wrecks occur upon our coast but that there are not more."

John Minturn—South of Mantoloking—February 15, 1846

Captain Dudley Stark of the three-masted packet ship *John Minturn*, which had recently departed New Orleans, sailed northeast along the New Jersey coast toward New York Harbor, the vessel's destination, with a cargo of cotton bales, tanned hides, barreled sugar, and pig lead valued at $84,000. On board the one-hundred-foot vessel were his wife, son, daughter, five passengers, twenty-two crewmen, and twenty seamen rescued from the ship *Cherokee*, which had foundered off Galveston a few weeks earlier. Thirty miles off the Atlantic Highlands, at about five in the afternoon, Captain Stark took aboard Thomas Freeborn, an experienced harbor pilot, to guide him into New York. It was Saturday, February 14, 1846, and a vicious nor'easter was headed toward the Jersey Shore.

Rain and high winds set in as the day wore on. After sundown, a north-east wind that had been blowing for several hours increased in velocity, buffeting the vessel. Freezing temperatures and snow made handling the ship difficult as it encountered what would prove to be one of the worst storms to strike the Jersey coast in decades. At about nine o'clock, with biting winds now at gale force, Freeborn instructed the crew to double-reef the topsails and furl the mainsail. "The foresail was hauled up but the running gear was rotten and the sail blew apart," recalled crewmember Steven Mitchell. "About midnight the pilot ordered the topsails to be close-reefed; but the first mate told him they were old and worn out and would be blown to pieces." As the crew struggled with the sails, the wind, now blowing between 50 and 60 miles per hour, pushed the *John Minturn* on a southerly course toward the Jersey coast.

The wind howled throughout the night. Near dawn the topsails blew away. After daylight the icy winds tore off the fore and aft sails, leaving the *John Minturn* at the gale's mercy. As the ship drifted ever closer to the beach, pilot and master made the only sensible decision: Instead of letting the wind push the ship broadside onto the outer bar, where huge waves could roll over her with crushing force, they hoisted a new topsail and ran directly for the beach. A few minutes later, the ship struck hard on the outer bar, about three hundred yards from shore, a mile south of Mantoloking. Huge waves and punishing winds lifted the ship onto the bar, then broke its back, hurling the wreck another one hundred feet closer to the mainland. Freeborn, who gave his greatcoat to the captain's wife and children in a heroic but vain attempt to shelter them from the icy rain, took charge, ordering the masts cut away to reduce the wind's impact.

A large crowd had meanwhile gathered on shore. Some were merely curious onlookers, others tried to help by launching boats, and, when that failed, wading out into the raging surf as far as they could, then throwing lines to the stranded vessel. On board the ship its crew worked frantically. "Exertion was made by the captain and mates to send a boat ashore with a heavy line," reported the *New York Herald.* "The first boat was stove.

The yawl was tried with better success, but the current carried her far to the southward, and the line was too short. They could not pay out from aboard, and as the boat was in the undertow, in the surf, they had to cut the line to save their lives." Leaded lines thrown by the crew were too short to reach the shore.

With Captain Stark now insensible from the numbing cold, Pilot Freeborn tried bravely to rally the crew and passengers. A boat launched with six crewmen aboard nearly capsized before it reached the shore safely. Further efforts to save those remaining alive on the ship were frustrated by the raging surf and floating wreckage. Those who could gathered on the forecastle and the foremast. "Night came on, and the stoutest were appalled," wrote the *Herald*. "The tide rose, and the ship broke up rapidly. The topgallant forecastle gave way, and Capt. Stark, with Freeborn, the women and children, all fell into the forward part of the ship; the broken timbers were tossed about for a moment, and the shrieks of the dying ceased."

Figure 14. The *John Minturn* struck a sandbar three hundred yards from shore a mile south of Mantoloking. Thirty-eight drowned, including the captain, his wife, son, and daughter, as well as harbor pilot Thomas Freeborn. From an 1846 Currier & Ives engraving.

Joseph Borden was one of those on shore who helped with the rescue. When the ship broke up at about eight o'clock at night, some eighteen hours after it had run aground, Borden and others stationed themselves along the beach to watch for survivors. "We stayed there with others until the ship parted, between eight and nine o'clock, and the top part came ashore," Borden later testified. "We took off six persons, part by boat and part by lines. I threw the line to one man to make it fast around him but he made it fast to the wreck. He appeared to be pretty much gone, but helped himself along by the rope as well as he could when a sea struck him and threw him clear of the wreck, but he held onto the rope with one hand. I ran down further into the surf and took hold of him; he was all under water except for one hand and arm. He caught me by the thigh under water, tearing my pantaloons with his other hand." With the help of another surfman, Borden managed to drag the man ashore.

Borden and his companions struggled for hours to save people clinging to the floating wreckage, throwing lines to them and easing them through the surf and on to the beach. The last to be rescued was John Sturgis, the second mate, who was so stiff from the cold he could barely help himself. "After we got off all the living men I went to the shanty, the rescued men were all there, and one man who was insensible, yet still alive," recalled Borden. "He seemed to have spasms; they tried to get a little warm drink down him but his teeth were so set that they could not. He died in about a quarter of an hour in great agony." Another surfman, Thomas Cook, was on the beach as the bodies washed ashore. "Many of them had been frozen stiff as they sat in a cramped position," he later said, "and I saw quite a number sitting so naturally on the sand that it was not until I held a lantern up to their faces that I knew they were dead."

The wreck of the *John Minturn* claimed thirty-eight lives, including those of Captain Stark and his family and Pilot Freeborn. Although ten ships came to grief on the Jersey coast that same day, the story of the *John Minturn* was the most appalling: stranded within sight of land, passengers and crew clung hopelessly to the wreckage amid howling wind and crashing waves while on shore surfmen and local farmers, some drawn by the opportunity to save lives, others by the fascination of seeing a ship torn apart by the breakers, seemed unable or perhaps unwilling to help them. The newspapers, staffed by reporters who had never tried to launch a rescue boat in the face of gale-driven waves littered with floating wreckage, charged the surfmen and local wreckmaster with indifference and incompetence. A greater effort, they proclaimed, could have saved more lives. "Accounts from the beach where the *John Minturn* and other vessels went ashore in the late storm," wrote the *Newark Daily Advertiser*, "represent the conduct of a set of unprincipled wretches who infest that portion of the Jersey shore, as disgraceful in the extreme." The paper headlined its story, "The Jersey Pirates." New York City papers claimed that the locals had robbed bodies washing up on the beach and then held the corpses for ransom. These "wreckers," the papers called them, were "a brutal tribe of the surf" who "danced with glee" as ships broke up and lives were lost.

Members of a commission appointed by New Jersey's governor investigated the *John Minturn* wreck thoroughly, visiting the scene of the disaster and taking the testimony of forty-three witnesses. The commissioners dismissed the hysterical newspaper stories as so much slander: "The records of the surf," they wrote in their report, "can show few more persevering, enduring, and courageous efforts to save the perishing passengers and seamen than were shown by the Monmouth surfmen on this occasion."

The men, women, and children who drowned when the *John Minturn* foundered on Mantoloking's shore are among countless thousands who lost their lives in the waters along New Jersey's coast. During the eighteenth and nineteenth centuries more than five hundred vessels—colonial merchantmen, Revolutionary War privateers, immigrant ships, and even steamships—sank off the coast. Between January 1846 and July 1848 alone, 122 vessels were wrecked. Perhaps the worst period of all was the months of December 1826 and January 1827, when two hundred ships broke up along the coast. People did not exaggerate when they called the coastal waters from Cape May Point to Sandy Hook a graveyard of ships.

Why were New Jersey's coastal waters so dangerous? Paralleling much of the coast, three hundred to eight hundred yards offshore, lurks a sandbar created by wave action. In some places not more than two feet beneath the surface, the bar is a trap for any vessel that dares to sail over it. The powerful nor'easters that roil the Atlantic Ocean during the winter months sent many a ship upon the bar, stranding them within sight of the safety of the beach even as the waves dashed them to pieces. This tragic loss of life prompted New Jersey Congressman William A. Newell to sponsor legislation establishing lifesaving stations along the Jersey Shore. After years of inattention, Congress finally acted in 1848, appropriating funds to set up eight stations on the coast between Sandy Hook and Little Egg Harbor. Each station was equipped with mortars capable of shooting a line to a stranded vessel and a life car, an unsinkable covered lifeboat invented by a Toms River boat builder that carried passengers and crew high above the dangerous waves. A wreckmaster and several helpers were assigned to patrol the coast during stormy weather, keeping a sharp eye out for vessels in distress. These stations marked the beginning of the U.S. Lifesaving Service, now part of the Coast Guard.

The Lifesaving Service proved its effectiveness in January 1850 when a heavy coastal storm drove the immigrant ship *Ayrshire* with 201 passengers aboard onto the shoals near Squan Beach. The mortar shot a line to the ship, heavier ropes were run out, and within a short time the life car was passing back and forth between the stricken vessel and the shore, bringing people to safety in twos and fours. Over the course of two days all but one of the passengers on the vessel were landed safely on the beach. The winter of 1849–50 also saw the surfboat rescue of some four hundred passengers and crew from the *Eudora* at Ludlam's Beach near Cape May.

The year 1853 brought more violent storms and harrowing shipwrecks. On January 14, the 1,200-ton New York packet ship *Cornelius Grinnell*, commanded by Captain A. J. Fletcher, was approaching the harbor with 270 passengers (English, German, and Irish immigrants) and an assorted cargo of bar iron, tin, oil, dry goods, and chalk. In the

Figure 15. A heavy coastal storm drove the *Ayrshire* onto the bar near Squan Beach. The Lifesaving Service, shown here at work on the beach, rescued all but one of the passengers. The ship was a total loss. From a contemporary engraving.

midst of a blinding snowstorm, Fletcher mistook one of the Highland's lights for that on Fire Island and a few minutes after 2:00 A.M. the ship struck the bar off Squan Beach. "The bar being composed of quicksand, the force of the wind and the sea caused her very soon to forge her way over on the beach," reported a newspaper. Captain Samuel Curtis, the local wreckmaster, and eight of his men were on the scene within hours, running lines and hawsers to the vessel. Once the ropes were secure, the surfboat went into operation; by 8:00 A.M. all of the passengers and crew had reached shore, "without one of them having received the slightest bruise." Another successful rescue took place on October 22, 1853, when the English ship *Western World* grounded off Spring Lake during a gale. The local wreckmaster and his men brought some six hundred grateful crew and passengers to shore by surfboat.

Not so fortunate were the passengers and crew of two immigrant vessels that foundered on the Jersey coast in 1854.

Powhattan—Beach Haven—April 15, 1854

The *Powhattan* was a 132-foot-long, three-masted, wooden-hulled packet bound to New York from Le Harve, France, with an estimated 250 to 340 passengers and crew aboard when it struck the outer bar just south of what is now Beach Haven on April 15, 1854. Built in Baltimore in 1836–37, the *Powhattan* had made numerous trips across the Atlantic, ferrying emigrants from Britain, Ireland, Holland, France, and Switzerland to America. Its last voyage departed Le Harve about March 1 with several hundred German emigrants packed tightly below decks. The captain was James Meyers of Baltimore, veteran of numerous ocean crossings. A vicious nor'easter pushed the helpless ship aground at about five in the evening at a place six miles south of the Harvey Cedars lifesaving station. "The spot where the *Powhattan* came ashore is about midway on Long Beach, between Barnegat Inlet and that of Egg Harbor," reported the *New York Herald*. "Between the shore and this beach is a capacious bay, not very deep, except in the channel, and is the resort in summer time of a number of anglers. Long Beach is about 20 miles long, and varies from one hundred to five hundred yards in width. It is from ten to twenty-five feet above the level of the sea, and can be seen a long distance from the shore. The ground is devoid of all vegetation, and being nothing more or less than an immense sand heap, glistening in the sun, it has no inhabitants, except two or three men stationed there by the government to render all the assistance in their power to shipwrecked mariners, thrown by the force of wind and tide upon its inhospitable shores."

Edward Jennings, the Long Beach Island wreckmaster, and his crew of four began patrolling the island at dawn, looking for wrecks. "On Saturday the wind blew with great violence from the northeast. The sea ran very high all day, and I supposed that there would be many a wreck along the coast from Barnegat to Egg Harbor," wrote Jennings in a statement he gave to the newspapers. "On Sunday morning I observed a ship of about 900 tons thumping on the bar about one hundred yards from the shore. I immediately sent those men who were with me to the government station-house, distant about six miles, for the life car, mortar, and other wrecking apparatus.

"During the day the ship's deck was crowded with passengers, and when the surf ran out I could get within seventy-five yards of the vessel, which I found out to be the ship *Powhattan*. . . ," said Jennings, describing the scene. "The surf ran mountains high; indeed I never saw such a sea in my life. Several persons now began to be swept overboard, when Capt. Meyers hailed me through his speaking trumpet and asked me for God's sake to try and save some of those who might happen to wash ashore."

Jennings searched along the beach but found only bodies. Meantime, his crew of four was struggling without success to bring equipment from the station house. So severe was the storm that "two of them fell down exhausted, and the whole party," according to the *Herald*, "were obliged to return [to the house] nearly frozen to death."

Desperate for help but aware that only one would-be rescuer stood on the beach, Captain Meyers again called out to Jennings to save any who reached the shore alive. "I replied that I would see to it, and went down about two hundred yards on the beach where the bodies were being washed ashore. Women and children came on shore first."

By this time the stricken vessel lay east southeast to the shore, its fore-mast torn off. "About 5 o'clock P.M. on Sunday, the ship keeled over to windward from the shore," said Jennings. "The sea then, of course, made a clean breach over her, and passengers began to be washed off in great numbers. The sea running mountain high, and completely hiding the vessel from my view, I could no longer hold any communication with the captain. I never saw him since. The main and mizzenmasts went by the board, and bodies appeared floating in the surf in great numbers. Some twenty-five bodies, mostly women, came on shore about a mile south of the wreck.

"About darkness the sea rose to a great height, and one large wave, fully a hundred feet high, struck the unfortunate vessel, and in one moment the hull was scattered into fragments which tossed wildly through the surf," recalled Jennings. "The shrieks of the drowning creatures were melancholy indeed, but I could render them no aid, as the sea ran so high I could not get near the unfortunate people. In a few moments all disappeared beneath the surface of the water, except a few fragments of the wreck. Never did I see such a sight in my life. Never do I remember witnessing such a dreadful gale or such high running sea. In many places it made complete breaches over the island, and carried, no doubt, many a poor fellow into the bay behind it." Jennings's men finally returned to the scene the next morning with a lifeboat, mortar, and the usual wrecking apparatus, "but it was too late, as all on board the ill-fated *Powhattan* had perished—not one remained to tell the fearful tale."

A reporter for the *Herald* who visited the beach where Wreckmaster Jennings and his men were gathering bodies and personal property washed up on the beach saw "about 30 trunks with goods in them . . . piled up together, among them several of the seamen's chests and the trunk of the first mate, Ambrose Kingsland Rogers, in which were several letters, pieces of poetry, a daguerreotype likeness, a lock of a lady's hair, and a number of shirts, underclothing, coats and pantaloons. All along the shore for ten miles were scattered the remnants of the chests and trunks of the passengers, many of them having names inscribed on the lids and sides. Feather beds, cooking utensils, empty casks and pieces of the vessel were to be seen on every side. Letters of the dead were scattered here and there, and bibles and prayer books lay glistening in the sun."

About 130 horribly mangled bodies washed ashore, including 21 children, many of them in their nightclothes. One young woman, "a beautiful looking creature, even as she lay in death," wore two rings—one plain and the other with a heart attached to it. They were marked "P.S." and "B.S.1854," probably wedding rings. "One man was found about 50 yards from the beach, upon the sand hills, with a child in his arms, " reported the *Herald*, "and from his condition it is supposed that he alone of all on board reached the shore alive, and crawling out of reach of the waves, in order to save his own life and that of the infant in his arms, fell down exhausted on the sand, and was frozen to death during the night. The child was firmly locked in his arms, quite dead, and appeared as if it had also died ashore from exposure."

Victims of the *Powhattan* disaster were buried in cemeteries in Smithville, Absecon, and Manahawkin. A monument dedicated to "The Unknown from the Sea" was erected in Manahawkin's Baptist Cemetery in 1904 to honor the victims of the *Powhattan* shipwreck.

The 2.5 million German, Irish, and English immigrants who poured into the United States in the 1850s crossed the Atlantic Ocean in sailing ships that one contemporary newspaper, the *New York Journal of Commerce*, condemned as "dammed plague ships and swimming coffins." After sailing to Europe laden with cargoes of rice, cotton, timber, and tobacco, the ships were hastily refitted with temporary flooring and bunks, then filled usually to capacity and beyond with hopeful immigrants bound for a new life in America. During a passage that could, depending on the weather, last anywhere from six to fourteen weeks, hundreds of passengers ranging in age from the newborn to grandparents in their seventies endured conditions that can only be described as horrendous.

Steerage passengers, crammed into double-decker berths six feet long by eighteen inches wide, had to provide their own mattresses and bedding. So overcrowded were most ships that people unable to stand the fetid atmosphere below decks slept in gangways or in flimsy wooden shacks built on the deck, where they were at great risk of being swept overboard by an errant wave. Sleeping areas were usually filthy; there was only a single privy for every one hundred people and just enough seats at the communal dining table for a quarter of the passengers at one time. Meals were mean and hasty affairs, frequently cooked on portable stoves erected on deck. Fresh food lasted a week or two at best. On one ship, as reported in Mary Cable's work, after two weeks out of port, "the potatoes gave out, the peas were musty, the meat and butter spoiled, and had to be thrown into the sea; the passengers lived on hard branny bread, prunes, and watery barley soup." Water was cut with vinegar to make it potable. Sanitation such as it was fell to the second mate, who dragooned all able-bodied passengers to help in the galley, swab the gangways, wash dirty laundry, and empty the chamber pots. Port workers boasted they could always tell that an immigrant ship had docked—by its stench.

Cholera and other diseases swept through the ranks of the passengers with frightening regularity; those who died were tossed overboard. Winter crossings were dreaded. When bad weather closed in, the ship's hatches were secured; no one was allowed on deck; and the passengers, most of them violently ill, were tossed about in the dark cramped quarters without fresh air or cooked food for days. There are no records of how many died on the passage to America or of the number of ships that never made port, lost to a violent mid-Atlantic storm or fire from a carelessly tended lantern. Other ships, like the *John Minturn* and the *Powhattan*, came within yards of safe haven before being dashed to pieces on the Jersey shore.

New Era—Deal Beach—November 13, 1854

Worst of the tragedies (and the best documented) was the wreck of the *New Era* on November 13, 1854, after it struck the sand bar off Deal Beach (now Seventh Avenue, Asbury Park) with a loss of about 215 lives.

Built in Bath, Maine, expressly for the immigrant trade, the three-masted sailing ship was commanded by its co-owner, Thomas Henry, assisted by a crew of twenty-nine: first mate, second mate, physician, steward, chief cook, carpenter, and twenty-three seamen. Twelve cooks were employed to prepare food for the passengers and crew. After an uneventful maiden journey to Europe, the *New Era* docked in Bremen, where an eager crowd of passengers awaited. Once six hundred tons of chalk and twenty thousand cubic feet of assorted merchandise were stowed aboard, the passengers climbed the gangplank to what was to be their home for the next forty-seven days. There were 384 of them, 10 of means housed in first and second cabin class, the remainder in steerage, all of them part of the great tide of German emigration then heading toward America. Passengers and crew had their last glimpse of Europe on September 28, 1854, as the *New Era* weighed anchor and sailed down the Weser River into the North Sea.

The Atlantic voyage was a nightmare almost from the start. Heavy seas and gale-force wind buffeted the ship. Nearly all of the passengers, most of whom had never been on a ship before, were continually seasick. At mid-ocean, a cholera epidemic broke out that took the lives of some forty passengers. Their bodies were hastily thrown into the sea. Louisa Heier, a twenty-five-year-old on her way from Prussia to Wisconsin to meet up with her fiancé, remembered the voyage as "full of the misery of sickness and want."

"My fellow passengers came from all parts of Germany," recalled Heier in an account in the *New York Daily Tribune*, and included farmers, mechanics, and tradesmen. Forty-two, she said, died on the ocean passage. "I cannot give a name to the disease of which they were the victims. I only know that, generally, they sickened at nightfall, and were cold before morning; those who died were, in every instance, young men from the rural districts, who were, on their arrival on shipboard, full of life and vigor; those unfortunates had been exhausted by want of proper food and fresh water—many of them having been reduced to drink of the water of the sea; there was scarcely any provisions, and those which were given us were of very bad quality, and not half cooked; we were compelled to hire cooks from among the passengers for ourselves." The ship's doctor, she added, was an insensitive brute.

"We had a very hard passage, with heavy west winds," Captain Henry told a newsman from the *New York Herald* after the disaster. "[A]bout the 20th of October, we shipped a sea that swept everything from the decks. The sea struck us fore and aft, and stove in the bulwarks, swept off the passengers' cooking range, killed two or three passengers, and disabled several others. The water passed into the main hatchway. . . . The gales continued very heavy, and the sea being so strong it strained the vessel so that she commenced leaking, and when reaching the United States coast, she leaked very bad. The leak was so rapid that it was requisite to keep one pump in operation all the time, prior to arriving here." The crewmen and able-bodied passengers who joined them at the pumps worked around the clock to no avail: Six feet of water filled the hold as the ship neared New York.

Strong southeast winds, torrential rain, and dense fog made navigation difficult. Calculating that he was off Long Island, Captain Henry put on extra sail and altered course southward to steer clear of the coast. Henry, it turned out, was utterly and tragically lost; instead of entering New York Bay and safety, the *New Era* was headed directly toward Deal Beach. Charles H. Griffen, an eighteen-year-old seaman, was on deck during the ship's final hours. "For three days previous to our going ashore, we had thick and heavy weather; in fact, during the whole passage we encountered violent head winds," Griffen told a *New York Daily Tribune* reporter after the wreck. "We took soundings at four o'clock, on Monday morning and found seventeen fathoms of water; again at five, when we were in fifteen fathoms of water. 5:30 we had shoaled to eleven fathoms. We reported the result of our sounding to the Captain, and the second mate came forward and told the watch that from the sand on the lead, we must be near the Jersey shore, and that we must keep a good lookout for land." So dense was the fog that the two lookouts posted could see no more than one hundred feet in any direction. Amazingly, Captain Henry went to his cabin, leaving an inexperienced second mate in charge.

On Monday, November 13, at about six in the morning, as the captain, much of the crew, and most of the passengers slept below, lookouts heard the dreaded sound of breakers just seconds before the *New Era* struck the bar with a resounding bump. "All were soundly asleep in the berths near me, when we were suddenly awoke, by feeling the ship was thumping heavily on the ground," related Johanna Heidenreich of Minden, Prussia. "We hurriedly dressed ourselves, but remained quietly below, while some of the men went on deck to inquire what was the matter. When they came back, in order to quiet our fears, I suppose, they said that nothing of any consequence had happened. But it was not long before the water rushed in, which at once created a general alarm. Soon the water came in so fast that many were drowned as they lay in their berths, before they could gather sufficient presence of mind to rise. There was now, consequently, a general rush for the deck." Once on the deck, the passengers held on as best they could, some taking shelter in the after cabin and some in the forecastle.

Gaspar Baberich, also from Prussia, told the *New York Herald* that he had been manning the pumps for four days straight. The ship grounded as he slept below, exhausted. "At first we did not realize the full extent of the danger, but we were soon made aware of it by the water rushing into the hold in a perfect torrent, and the breaking of the spray over the deck as she swayed to and fro in the heavy sea." When the deck planking began to give way, said Baberich, "portions of the cargo were forced up from the hold, tearing up the planks. Several of the passengers were crushed to death between barrels, casks, and boxes, and were afterwards swept overboard by the waves in a horribly mutilated condition. . . . A terrible scene of excitement ensued on board among the passengers, some of whom clung to the sailors with a terrible tenacity, imploring them to save them."

A northerly current swung the ship broadside to the beach, the worst location possible. Wind-driven waves broke high over the stranded vessel, drowning some and sweeping others over the side. In less than an hour the shattered vessel filled with water and sank. With the deck now at sea level, surviving passengers and crew scrambled for safety. Some of the men climbed out on to the yards and bow sprint. Johanna Heidenreich took shelter in the forecastle. "For from two to three hours we managed to protect ourselves against the fury of the raging waves, wet to the skin, however, and almost reckless through despair," Heidenreich told the *Herald*. "During the time the bulwarks and a part of the forecastle were washed away, and about nine o'clock in the morning, the forecastle, where I had taken shelter, with some 20 others, began to break up, when I left it with my poor mother." The waves repeatedly washed over Johanna and her mother, "and in spite of all I could do, my dear mother was knocked down two or three times as we endeavored to make our way to the rigging, where we thought we might find some shelter. At last, however, exhausted with fright, fatigue, and the continued dashing of the waves over her, she fell down on the deck, and before I had any time to render her any assistance, a large wave carried her over the side. I never saw her again."

Those carried overboard by the waves drowned in the churning water. Louisa Heier's fate, as reported in the *Daily Tribune*, was different. After retrieving a purse containing two hundred dollars from her trunk, she rushed up the steps to the deck, "but at the very moment I had emerged from the steerage an immense wave burst over the deck, and carried me with it into the sea. As I was thus hurried overboard, however, I had presence of mind sufficient to enable me to seize a rope that lay upon the planks near me, and clung tenaciously to it. As the waves cast me back toward the ship, a broken spar floated near me; I disengaged my right hand from the rope, and clung with my arm around this gift of divine mercy. . . . Thus maintaining my hold upon the rope and the spar, I was cast back and forth by the waves, and it was during this terrible episode of my misfortune, that my body was bruised by being thrown violently against the side of the ship."

Trapped alongside the ship, Louisa was tossed around by the waves for more than an hour. No one on the ship noticed her, "every one on board of the vessel being too much filled with his own danger . . . ; and not the least part of my anguish was that while thus numbed with cold and wounded I was compelled to listen to the loud, loud cries of terror which burst from the despairing crowd who thronged the rigging of each of the masts. It was then raining, the wind was high, and the sea running in immense channels. Suddenly the rope by which I had been secured to the ship parted, and I drifted away, shrieking loudly for assistance. I became almost unconscious with terror. I felt the huge waves breaking over me, and though from the natural instinct of selfpreservation, I clung yet more closely to the spar, it seemed to me that my hold was gradually relaxing, and I must inevitably perish." The tide carried Louisa toward the beach. When she neared the shore, a man who saw her struggling in the waves rallied about twenty onlookers; they formed a human chain, waded into the roiling surf and pulled Louisa from the wreckage. She was the only passenger to go overboard who made land safely.

Still clinging precariously to the sunken ship, Johanna Heidenreich worked her way to the shrouds, which offered some protection from the waves. "I had now partially recovered from my first fright, and looking round I saw my brother, his wife, and little child crowded with others into the place where the coals had been stored away. Seizing a favorable lull between two waves, I joined my brother, who had repeatedly called to me, and who, like myself, had seen our mother drown. How I was saved I cannot tell. When I recovered my self-possession again, I found that the wave had torn all my clothing off my back except my chemise. I sat for hours next to my brother [Fritz], with the water continually dashing over us. Every moment we expected would be our last."

Eight hours after the *New Era* foundered, said Heidenreich, "my brother's child was torn away, by a succession of large waves from the enfeebled grasp of his wife. It was rapidly swept out of sight. Soon after this occurred, I noticed that two men had been drowned close to us, although they seemed to be well sheltered from the fierce waves, but the repeated dashing of water over us had at last drowned them. The waves eventually carried them away too. I could see men, strong men, springing from the rigging during the intervals between the waves, in vain attempts to rescue wife and child, crying continually, 'My wife—my child!' in tones that, distressed as I already was by my own griefs and losses, penetrated my heart. As we sat we could see the bodies of many of our fellow passengers, tossed about on the raging waters . . . in masses, as if when first launched into the waves they had grappled with one another, and so drowned."

Heinrich Bruggermann was another passenger who took refuge in the rigging after abandoning the forecastle. The *New York Daily Tribune* also carried his story: "The forecastle was built above the deck, and while I remained seated in one of the berths, the waves carried away both its sides.

The water being already two feet deep there, I thought it better to leave, and so climbed up to the fore top-yard. The swell, however, was so great that many of the waves still broke over myself and the others there. I consequently came down and got out on the bowsprit. I found about fifty passengers there before me. But every now and then some huge wave would wash several of them overboard. Determined to do the best I could to save my life, I took refuge on the top of the forecastle, but being at last driven from my position there, I again climbed upon the foremast, going, however, much higher than I had done before—as high as the fore top-gallant yard. I could see that some people were being washed overboard nearly every moment. In the course of the day I saw as many as one hundred and sixty passengers drowned."

In his cabin when the ship grounded, Captain Henry rushed on deck, giving orders to brace around the yards in an effort to back the vessel off the shoal. "After several ineffectual attempts we found this impossible, as every sea was driving her further on the beach," related Seaman Griffen. "Orders were then given to clear away the boats. The first boat was manned by the first and second officers and three of the crew, and started for the shore with a line, but in consequence of the line being too short they did not succeed in getting it ashore, as they were compelled to let it go, although the boat reached the beach. The second boat was then lowered and manned for the purpose of trying to get another line on shore, but the line became entangled on board the ship, and the boat was obliged to let it go also. Our last boat (the long boat) was cleared away and got over the side, to renew the attempt to get a rope to the beach. That boat was large enough to carry about 25 or 30 persons; five or six of the crew got into her to bale her out. At this time the captain was in the mizzen rigging, on the starboard side, and gave us orders about the boat. Six of the crew were in her baling, when a sea struck her and her painter parted. She was carried away from the ship, and those who were in her were obliged to make for the shore. The ship's surgeon, Dr. Papenhusen, attempted to get into her by lowering himself on a line, but was too late, and the sea washed him off, and he was drowned.

"The captain told the people to remain quiet, and they would all get ashore," continued Griffen, "but they heeded him not, but kept crying for assistance. The captain also shouted at the top of his voice for help from the shore. The poor people on board were being continually swept off into the sea. The whole of the rigging on the starboard side was filled with them, probably to the number of 200 souls."

The disaster's only saving grace was its location a few hundred yards from the home of Abner Allen, the volunteer keeper of the Deal Beach Lifesaving Station since 1848. Awakened by the ship's bell and distress gun, Allen roused himself and some neighbors and within an hour a handful of men had gathered on the beach opposite the wreck. Allen had his surfboats at the ready but lacked the manpower to launch them. By eleven in the morning, as news of the wreck spread up and down the coast, over a hundred people gathered on the beach; some brought additional boats. Pushing off into the turbulent surf, however, proved to be impossible. Allen and Edward Wardell, an agent of the American Coast Wrecking Company, set up their mortar gun, firing four shots toward the ship. The fourth line caught in the rigging and was made fast by the remaining crewmembers.

"After several ineffectual attempts, the people on shore succeeded in firing a shot over us, and sending a line across our fore royal stay, and a man on the end of the flying jib boom caught it," continued Griffen. "The captain made it fast by the fore stay, and all of us hauled the lifeboat from the shore to the ship. The captain got into the fore chains, and was followed by a part of the crew. The boat having capsized several times in coming to us, was full of water, and the captain ordered some of the crew to get in and bale her out. As soon as they got in he jumped overboard, and scrambled into the boat, leaving five of the crew and his passengers on board. As soon as he got into the boat he cried out to the people on the beach to haul him on shore. When the passengers saw the captain leaving his ship, ten or twelve of them jumped overboard, and four of them got into the boat—the remainder were drowned.

"The coast people hauled the boat toward the shore, but she capsized three times in going, and only the captain, three of the crew and one of the passengers got ashore in safety—the remainder were drowned. On her way to the shore the line connecting the shore and the ship parted, and we were left again to despair." About three in the afternoon Allen and his crew were able to shoot another line into the rigging, but it caught in the foretopsail brace, beyond the reach of anyone still alive on the ship.

The steam tug *Achilles* left Sandy Hook for the scene of the wreck about 9:30 in the morning, inching its way through the same dense fog bank that had enveloped the *New Era*. "About [3:00 P.M.] we came in sight of her, lying broadside to the beach, heading to the southward, with her fore, main, and mizzen topsails closereefed still standing," reported Captain Elias Smith, a passenger on the *Achilles*, whose account appears in Julius Sachse's collection of articles. "On reaching her, she proved to be level with the water and full, and the swell breaking in heavy surges across her decks. We had already passed many pieces of the wreck, and half a mile further on we saw the body of a little child, apparently about four or five years old, and in quick succession also that of a man, stripped of clothing, and others with clothes on—four or five bodies in all. As we approached the wreck, so as to get a nearer view, a most harrowing spectacle met the eyes.

"The jibboom, rigging and top of the ship, fore and aft, were filled with human beings closely packed together, and clinging to each other, and to the ropes, while the ship surged to and fro with each returning wave, which broke into spray far into the rigging and over the ship, drenching, and suffocating the passengers, while the poor creatures filled the air with the most soulharrowing and pitiful outcries for assistance. On the beach were some two hundred persons, gathered in groups, apparently consulting as to how to act, while others sat leisurely upon the gunwale of the boats, which the heavy surf rendered it certain destruction to launch.

"We saw several boats upon the shore, apparently well adapted for the purpose, and a crowd of persons dragging along a lifeboat toward the beach, where it was left, and no further attempt was made to launch it. We saw no line from the ship to the shore, and no lifecar. From the fact that what appeared to be the ship's boat was lying on the beach, we judged that the officers and crew, or most of them, must have landed or been thrown ashore in her. The tide was now about at its full, the wind had died away, and a slight breeze sprang up from off shore, which greatly increased our hopes that the swell would go down with the tide, and render it possible for the boats to be launched from shore. As to ourselves, we found we could do nothing." The *Achilles*, chartered by maritime underwriters to assist vessels that had come ashore in distress, had no surfboats or life preservers nor, said Captain Smith, "a piece of cork big enough to float a drowning dog.

"Still hoping for a movement toward launching the boats from shore, we continued painful spectators of the scene, ringing our bell to encourage them, and beckoning to them on the shore to launch the boats. When our wheels were put in motion to adjust the position of the steamer, the passengers, apparently fearing we were about to leave them, would rend the air with imploring cries, while others tolled the ship's bell, the sounds of which were borne to us above the wailing of the surf that swept over the ship.

"We were near enough," continued Smith, "to distinctly see women holding their little ones with one hand, while the other, bleached by the spray, clung with a death grip to the ratlines on which they stood, only one or two in the mizzen rigging, having on but a shirt. On the forecastle there stood a few moments ago a group of four clinging to the stay, but they are now gone—a heavy swell has probably swept them away. Men have been seen to fall from the jibboom into the surf.

"Thus we have looked on, unable to approach the ship. Captain Reynolds [of the *Achilles*] twice hailed them on the shore, and asked them to launch the boats, as the surf, to us, seemed to be now sufficiently smooth to do so on the lee side of the ship. Finding that we could do nothing, and as the sun went down, seeing the boats hauled back upon the beach, we left to procure life boats, making signals to the wreck that we would return immediately." Meantime, the steamboat *Leviathan* also arrived opposite the wreck, but like the *Achilles* it had no lifeboats.

Several hundred people milled about on the beach, some merely curious sightseers, others there to render aid if they could. Heavy surf pounded the shore, frustrating all efforts at rescue. Although only a hundred yards separated the surfmen from the stranded passengers, there was nothing anyone could do to help.

From his perch in the rigging, Seaman Griffen could see the *Achilles* and *Leviathan* several hundred yards away. "About ten o'clock on Monday night, a boat from a steamboat came to us, within hailing distance, and asked how we got along," said Griffen. "I replied, we should do very well till morning if the ship held together, but I did not think she would last so long. The captain of the boat told us to hold on and he would soon be off to us with a lifeboat and assistance. We got a line ready for lowering ourselves into the boat, and he returned in about half an hour and hailed us again to know how we were. We asked him to come along and take us in, but he waited for fifteen minutes and found it impossible to come, as the sea was so boisterous."

About eight o'clock, the men on the beach built a huge bonfire, which they kept burning all night. If the fire warmed the rescuers, said Griffen, it did nothing for those desperately clinging to the wreck. "About twelve o'clock the sea began to break over our place of shelter on the boom, and we got up onto the forestay and into the foretop. All this time the deck was strewn with dead bodies which the sea washed to and fro against the frames and bulwarks and the rolling spars and rubbish, mangled terribly. A cold westerly wind arose about eight o'clock on Monday evening; the night was very bleak, the blast piercingly cold, and many of the emigrants benumbed and frozen, lost their hold and dropped from the shrouds into the sea and were drowned. Others, exhausted, hung by their legs in the rigging, too feeble to longer maintain their hold, and so perished from suffocation."

When it became dark Allen and his men were forced to abandon any further rescue attempts until dawn the next day. Toward morning the gale moderated; at first light, Allen's men launched their surfboats. Drenched by the waves, almost naked and despairing for her life, Johanna Heidenreich had given up all thoughts of rescue when, at about seven in the morning, she heard someone cry out, "A boat! A boat!"

"I managed to creep along the yardarm so that I could look upon the shore. To my great joy I saw the shape of three boats. They came alongside, taking advantage of the short intervals between the breaking of the waves. Many of the men, pale and worn out, dropped from the yards and rigging, and got safely into the first boat. Others were taken in the second, and at length I came along, in the third." Johanna's brother, Fritz, and his wife were also rescued. Survivors were brought to shore in groups of six or ten, and by 10:00 A.M. all the living had been taken off the wreck.

At about 4:00 P.M. on Tuesday, the *Achilles* returned to the scene of the disaster. "The ship lay about three hundred yards from the shore, on the outer bar, her deck level with the water, and the sea washing over her continually," wrote Captain Smith. "The fore, main, and mizzen topsails were still set, as when she went on, treble reefed. The other sails appeared to be loosely clewed up, and rent in many places. In the main shrouds, the body of a female was still visible, nearly nude, her arms and legs thrust through the crossings. The planking of the bulwarks was all torn off, and the sea belched every moment through the frame of the bulwarks, like the smoke from a frigate's guns when firing a broadside."

Captain Smith, along with Captain Browne of the *Hector*, another ship at the scene, sat anxiously in the *Achilles*'s surfboat as its crew rowed toward the hulk. "Watching an opportunity, as a spent wave receded, we leaped into the mizzen rigging. Such a spectacle as the decks of the *New Era* then presented we hope never to be called to witness again. The forecastle was beaten in, and the top of the poopcabin on the larboard side had a large hole in it that the waves had made. The deck had been swept of everything. The frames of the bulwarks stood above the waves, like the fleshless ribs of a leviathan, while protruding through them were the bodies of men, women, and children, all of them naked, or but partially covered with the clothes they had on when asleep in their berths. But the most awful sight of all was directly below our feet. There, between the side of the poopcabin and the mizzen chains about a score of corpses, all stark, stiff, and cold, lay in every conceivable attitude of agony. Maimed, crushed, and bruised, with eyes washed from their sockets, with teeth set like vises, and every feature fearfully convulsed; there, promiscuously heaped together, were old men whose race had nearly run, young maidens, just blooming into womanhood, and babes whose lives were measured but by weeks. Every age and sex had its representative here, and told in ghastly types how much humanity may suffer."

Captain Browne picked his way cautiously along the top of the bulwarks toward the main mast in order to take down a women's body hanging there. "With some difficulty he disentangled her stiffened limbs from the shrouds, and gently lowered her . . . by a rope into the surf boat. . . . The people on shore silently bore off the body of the young girl, that had so long lain stiffening in the rigging, that it might be prepared for Christian burial."

Survivors were given shelter by Allen and his neighbors, provided food and warm clothing, and then taken to New York City where R. A. Witthaus of the German Society met them at the dock. The sick and injured—"death-like, as their limbs were chilled, their eyes sunken"— were sent to city hospitals while the able-bodied were put up at the German Tavern on Greenwich Street. Two of those rescued lost little time beginning a new life in America: Peter Kopp, said to be "a fine appearing young German," and his fiancée, Theresa Wolfe, both of Bavaria, were married as soon as they arrived in the city. The total number drowned was never officially established, but most sources agreed that between 210 and 215 lost their lives in the wreck. Surprisingly, only two members of the crew, a steward and the physician, were among the dead.

The sad task of removing bodies from the wreck continued for several days. Some bodies washed ashore as far north as Sandy Hook, others were gathered from nearby beaches. Most were unidentifiable. A January 1855 gale churned up the wreckage, depositing another thirteen mutilated corpses on Deal Beach.

Allegations that the captain and crew had been careless in their handling of the vessel surfaced almost immediately. When it was learned that all but two crewmembers had survived, that the captain and mates had escaped the vessel on the ship's boats and that only five crewmen had stayed aboard to assist the passengers, many wanted to charge the ship's officers with criminal negligence. Captain Allen, a veteran of many such wrecks, suggested as much in a statement he gave to the *New-York Daily Times*, where he pointed out that within several hours of the grounding "the crew had effected a landing on the beach, with six passengers, in the three boats belonging to the ship. The First Mate came in the first boat, with four or five sailors. The second boat, I believe, contained no passengers. The third boat was manned by the crew, and also contained a few passengers. The fourth was the life-boat, and landed with the captain and some of the crew."

"The probable cause of the disaster is a subject which is engaging the conversations of all who have visited the beach," reported the *Daily Times*. "It is attributed by many to official neglect of duty. First, it is stated among the passengers that neither the Captain nor the Mate were upon the deck at the time the vessel struck; that the captain was in his cabin asleep, it being the mate's watch, and that the latter had forsaken his post and had been below for some time."

Captain Henry defended himself, claiming he was only in the lifeboat helping to bail it out when panicky passengers crowded aboard, the line parted, and he ended up on the beach. Henry blamed his crew, telling reporters his men had "deserted" the sinking vessel. The first mate, George Jordan, sided with the captain, saying to the newspapers that stories that Henry was among the first to come ashore were "entirely untrue. He was the last, on the day of the wreck, to leave the ship, and did not do so till all hope of rescuing either ship or passengers had been abandoned."

Passengers interviewed by reporters told an entirely different tale. Gaspar Baberich of Ham, Prussia, described for a *New York Herald* newsman: "a terrible scene of excitement . . . on board among the passengers, some of whom clung to the sailors with a terrible tenacity, imploring them to save them. The sailors endeavored to lighten the vessel by cutting away the masts, but failing in this they got out the boats, determined to save their own lives. The passengers made a rush for the first boat when it was lowered, but the sailors stood before it with drawn knives, and threatened to kill any who attempted to get into it."

Reporters hurried to the German Tavern as the bedraggled survivors arrived. A native of Hesse Cassel, Wilhelm Schmelz, told one newsman from the *Daily Times* that he was on deck boiling water for some coffee when the ship struck the bar. "The second mate was on deck at the time, but not the captain or the first mate. Immediately after we struck I saw the mate come out of the cabin in his drawers." Schmelz claimed that Jordan "during the entire passage, had been upon terms of great intimacy with the wife of a German chemist who was on board. . . . This fact was a matter of common conversation, and the fact that the chemist's wife and the chief mate slept together was not attempted to be kept secret." In fact, charged Schmelz, First Mate Jordan was not the only officer who might have been dallying below decks as the ship headed for disaster. "It was stated . . . that Captain Henry had also a German girl in the cabin, whom he had given a free passage to America, and with whom he was living upon terms of similar intimacy. Similar conduct was charged against the second mate." Other passengers, including Sussmann Heinemann, Louise Heier, and August Steinecker, confirmed the story.

Summing up "what appear to be the facts in this case," the *New York Herald* spoke for many when it charged that the *New Era* had been "deserted by the captain, mates, and nearly all hands. It does not appear that they made the least effort to save the passengers—until safely ashore themselves. They may be able to clear themselves from the strong suspicion of cowardice and desertion which is now so freely spoken of them; but until they do, we fear that the frightful homicide . . . will be laid to their charge."

Despite the public outcry, city and state officials remained silent. "It is beginning to be clear that neither the General Government nor our local authorities intend to have any investigation in the causes and circumstances of the loss of . . . the *New Era*," complained the *Daily Times*. So far as the government was concerned, charged the newspaper, the "dreadful disaster excites [no] more attention than the harmless upsetting of an ash cart in Broadway." Calling such inaction a "disgrace to our pretended civilization," the *Daily Times* demanded action. "A large ship is run ashore at the very entrance to our harbor, there, within a few hundred yards of the land, two or three hundred human beings, men, women, and children, are left helpless upon the wreck by the desertion of the captain and crew . . . and yet no man lifts a finger—no coroner, prosecuting attorney, grand jury, or other functionary of the law, stirs a step towards making inquest into this wholesale slaughter."

New York law enforcement authorities eventually yielded to public opinion, convening a federal grand jury that began hearing testimony in January 1855. Although the grand jury found that "on the part of Capt. Thomas J. Henry there was neglect and a want of vigilance necessary to guard and protect the lives of those who were under his care," no indictment could be handed up because, it said, no laws had been broken.

Once the town coroner completed his inquest, more than two hundred bodies placed in rough wooden boxes were buried in a common grave in the West Long Branch Methodist Cemetery. The New Era Association, organized by Germans living in the area, dedicated an imposing granite monument at the site in 1892. Association members cared for the grave for many years, determined to preserve the memory of those so tragically lost on Deal Beach.

New York—North of Barnegat Inlet—December 20, 1856

Little more than two years after the wreck of the *New Era* another immi-grant ship, the *New York*, bound from Liverpool to New York City with a crew of 27 and about 280 passengers, mostly Irish, went ashore on the Jersey coast. Commanded by Captain Alex McKinnon, the *New York* had suffered a rough passage across the Atlantic, sailing through a succes-sion of westerly gales. During all of his twenty-five years at sea, Captain McKinnon told George Newbrook, a cabin passenger from Liverpool, "he had never experienced so much rough weather on one voyage."

"Just after sundown on Friday night we got a fairer wind than we had had on the whole passage," remembered another cabin passenger, John Carr of Birmingham. "We were all in very high spirits, and retired to rest with cheerful hopes." Unable to sleep, Carr went on deck to join the captain, who was standing on the poop with a telescope in hand, trying to make out a light he spied to the west. Despite his many years at sea, McKinnon was lost. What he thought was a ship's light turned out to be Old Barney, the Barnegat Light, built in 1834 on the south side of Barnegat Inlet to guide mariners to the bay. "The weather at the time was clear, and the moon was just about rising," reported George Newbrook, in a sur-prisingly charitable mood despite the wreck. "How the vessel could go on shore under such circumstances appears somewhat unaccountable." The *New York* hit the sand bar head-on about 150 yards from shore, about two miles north of the lighthouse.

"At midnight we were all awakened by the shock of the ship's striking; she quivered and trembled as though she was going to tumble to pieces," remembered Carr. "A thrill of horror ran through the passengers; they leaped from their births and dressed, trembling with fear; some fell upon their knees, and cried aloud, 'Lord have mercy upon us'; others remained calm, having confidence in the ability of the captain and officers that they would do all that could be done to save us. In the steerage there was fearful confusion, shrieking, hallooing, howling, weeping, moaning, praying, groaning. So terrible I scene I have never before witnessed. . . .

"Immediately on striking the sails were reversed and every possible effort made to back her off." After an hour the crew, realizing the ship was stuck fast in the sand, began firing rockets hoping to attract the attention of anyone on shore. When the ship began to take on water, the crew manned the pumps, giving up the effort after several hours when the water began gaining on them. At dawn a boat was launched, but was forced against the side of the ship and stove in. A second boat succeeded in reaching the beach with the second mate, five seamen, and five able-bodied passengers. Another boat filled with ten passengers and five crew also managed to gain the beach. Frustrated by the inability of crew members on shore to rig a line to the ship, Captain McKinnon decided to take matters into his own hands, took another boat, several female passengers, and some crewmen and landed on the beach successfully. McKinnon's effort to get a line to the ship failed as well.

"The condition of those on deck at this junction was most deplorable," reported the *New York Herald*. "The side of the vessel nearest to the land was crowded with human beings of both sexes and of all ages, and as they stood there imploring the assistance of those on shore with almost frantic gesticulations, the spray dashed over them in drenching showers. The ship was laboring heavily all this time, and sinking deeper in her sandy bed, while each wave that struck her made her tremble from stem to stern."

Meantime, wreckmaster John Allen had spied a vessel on the bar, gathered his surfmen, and arrived at the scene to set up a mortar. "The first ball that was fired from the mortar was rendered useless from the breaking of the chain which connects it with the line," wrote the *Herald*. "A second ball was fired, but it was equally ineffectual from the same cause. The third, however, was more successful, and the line was seized by those on board and firmly secured. A life car was run along the line to the ship, the surf rendering it impossible for any boat to pull out from

Figure 16. Titled "Hauling in the Life-Car, Seabright," this engraving depicts members of the U.S. Lifesaving Service rescuing passengers from a stranded vessel using an enclosed lifeboat. From *Frank Leslie's Illustrated Newspaper*, February 8, 1873.

the shore. One by one the passengers were transferred from the ship to the car and landed safely, and in this way some sixty persons were taken off the wreck." Rescue efforts were suspended when the sun went down. About seventy-five passengers and crew now found themselves stranded on the beach, cold, wet, and hungry. Some made their way to the nearby lifesaving house, a tiny shack with a small stove. Others huddled on the beach without protection from the wind and spray. All passed a miserable night, catching what sleep they could.

On Sunday morning rescue work resumed. The wind had died down, the sea was calmer, and three surfboats were put into service to take off the remaining passengers and crew. Early in the morning Captain McKinnon and several of his officers returned to the wreck to supervise the work. "During the absence of the officers, some of the sailors . . . behaved most riotously," said the *New-York Daily Times*. "They rifled the between decks, broke into the store-room, and seized the liquor. On the return of the officers an assault was made upon them, and the captain in the melee was beaten over the head with a heavy iron pot, and received eight large wounds on the scalp, from the effects of which he is in a precarious situation. One of his eyes was nearly knocked out, and he will probably lose it." The mutiny ended when the officers drew their pistols.

Sunday evening found most of the passengers, crew, and surfmen still on the beach, "in a most deplorable condition . . . , without food and destitute of shelter . . . ; men, women, and children of all ages, huddled together for warmth and cowered upon the bare sand before the December blast," reported the *West Jerseyman*, a newspaper published in Camden. "Here and there, a little driftwood was gleaned, or a few stray sticks gathered and kindled into flame. These ghostly fires flickered faintly, but for a while rendering more apparent the utter desolation of the scene, and then went out. That was a dark and fearful night." No one had eaten for nearly three days and none had warm clothing. "It is no wonder then that hungry, debilitated, and hopeless, they sank on the sand in blank despair." Although many suffered frostbite, all managed to survive the night. On Monday morning a group walked to Point Pleasant, others eventually found transportation to Freehold. A steamboat sent by the New York underwriters finally arrived, taking the remaining passengers to their destination.

Built at New York in 1839 for the Black Ball Line of sailing packets that plied between Liverpool and New York and back again, the 152-foot-long *New York* was described as an "exceptionally handsome vessel" for its time. Retired by Black Ball in 1854 when it was considered too small and outdated, it entered the immigrant trade, sailing between England and

America. Why the ship foundered on the Jersey coast so far south of its destination remains a mystery. To the great good fortune of the three hundred souls on board, it sailed under the command of a captain who understood his duty. In the wreck of the *New York* only one person lost his life—one of the sailors who assaulted the captain. On gaining the beach, he froze to death and was buried where he died, in the sand.

Vizcaya and Cornelius Hargraves—Off Barnegat Bay—October 30, 1890

The *Vizcaya* was the pride of the Compañía Transatlántica Española, a Spanish company that owned a fleet of more than sixty ships operating between Spain, New York, Cuba, Central America, and the Philippines. Built in London in 1878, with an average speed of fourteen knots (faster when its 850-horsepower steam engines were augmented by canvas), it was steel-hulled, three-masted, and 287 feet long. Rated 100 A1 by Lloyds of London, the ship was, said the newspapers, "in every way a good vessel," one of the favorite boats of the CTE.

After a boiler explosion in 1887 killed virtually every crewman standing night watch, the ship was "elegantly refitted" for the American trade. The *Vizcaya* featured a handsome one-hundred-foot-long on-deck dining room, a smoking saloon for the male passengers, and a ladies' parlor decorated in white and gold velvet and plush with marble ornamentation. There were accommodations for two hundred first-, second-, and third-class passengers in equally luxurious staterooms. The ship was valued at $500,000.

The *Vizcaya* steamed out of New York Harbor at one o'clock in the afternoon of October 30, 1890, bound for Havana with a crew of seventy-seven, sixteen passengers (including four children), and a cargo of miscellaneous merchandise valued at $350,000. Among the passengers were three Cuban millionaires, Ramon Alvarez, a cigar exporter; Manuel Calvo, a sugar merchant; and Juan Pedro, who owned two sugar plantations on the island. Calvo and Pedro were also large stockholders in the

CTE. On the bridge stood Captain Francisco Cunill, a veteran of more than twenty years at sea, and a member, like his fellow officers, of the Spanish Royal Naval Reserve. The weather at departure was clear, the mood on board relaxed.

Six hours later and sixty miles into its voyage, the *Vizcaya* lay at the bottom of the ocean, the victim, reported the *New York Herald*, of "a disaster to make the blood run cold with horror, numbering among its victims sweet women and innocent children." Struck amidships by a coal schooner, the steamer sank within minutes, taking to their death all sixteen passengers and fifty-three of the crew. It was, said the *New York Times*, "an unexplainable accident."

Three days before the *Vizcaya* cast off, the *Cornelius Hargraves*, a 211-foot-long double-decked centerboard schooner cleared Philadelphia's harbor with a heavy load of coal bound for Fall River, Massachusetts. Sturdily built in Maine of oak and yellow pine for its owner and captain, John F. Allen of Fall River, the *Cornelius Hargraves* was a trim ship, only thirteen months in service. Considered a "very fast sailer," it carried a big spread of canvas on its four masts. A seasoned crew of ten manned the vessel as it sailed north along the Jersey coast.

A hardheaded Yankee captain and an inexperienced Spanish third mate was the fatal combination that put the two ships on a collision course, sending both to the bottom of the ocean in the busy sea-lanes eight miles due west of the Barnegat Light. Amazingly, a lookout on the *Cornelius Hargraves* had spotted the *Vizcaya* fifteen minutes before the collision, more than enough time and distance to avoid disaster. "I had finished supper Thursday night and came on deck about 7 o'clock," the schooner's second mate Angus Walker told the *New York Tribune*. "I saw the *Vizcaya* about five miles away. Her lights were plainly visible. We were sailing at the rate of about eight knots an hour and neared the Spanish vessel rapidly." Described by the *Tribune* as an "intelligent man about twenty-three," Walker sent up a warning flare. When the *Vizcaya* failed to change course, he summoned Captain Allen on deck.

"About 7 o'clock in the evening Mate Walker, who was in charge of the deck, came to the companion way and called down that there was a steamer showing a green light on our port bow," First Mate Henry Perring told the *Tribune*. "The captain was sitting in the cabin reading, and I was lying in my bunk, but when the mate called out we both went on deck. About an eighth of a mile away was the green light of a steamer. When the captain saw her he exclaimed, 'What the devil does the fellow mean?' Turning to Walker he asked, 'Have you shown him a torch?' He then ordered Walker to go forward and make a flare. The steamer paid no attention to the light, and as we had the right of way we kept on." Under the rules of navigation, the green light they saw meant that they should stay their course, but without getting into a collision situation.

"It seemed as if the people on the steamer were all either drunk or asleep," said Mate Perring. "They did not swerve a hair's breadth from their course, but simply rushed down upon us. We then saw that a crash must come. Captain Allen was as cool as possible. When he saw that the steamer took no notice of our torch, he shouted at the top of his voice to the man at the wheel: 'Hard a-starboard. Put your helm hard a-starboard.' This action, if it had been responded to by the steamer, might have saved us; but, to our surprise, the *Vizcaya* at that moment swerved right across our bows. I stood as if paralyzed for a moment and then I grasped the rigging and shut my eyes. Then came the shock. There was a crash, following by a ripping of timber and falling of spars. We drove almost through the steamer, right abaft her foremast." Sailing at full speed, the *Cornelius Hargraves* smashed into the *Vizcaya* at an acute angle, penetrating deep into the steamer's coal bunkers, its pointed bowsprit sweeping along the deck, tearing away rigging, boats and deck fittings.

The *Vizcaya*'s second officer, Francisco Covas, had just finished dinner and was below-decks talking with the purser. Captain Cunill was in the smoking room chit-chatting with the passengers. On the bridge was Third Officer Francisco Morillas.

"The time was slipping away pleasantly enough, when suddenly we heard the whistle blow sharply and the bell in the engine room signal to reverse engines," Covas told a *New York Herald* reporter. "The officers of the ship rushed to the deck. Captain Cunill ascended the bridge and took command, but was unable to change the order of fate. The schooner was upon us, and struck us amidships, almost head on. The crash of the metal and timbers and the shrieks, groans, prayers and curses of the passengers and crews was horrible."

The *Vizcaya* forged ahead. "The schooner, which was waveling about, continued in the other direction. Its bowsprit carried away a portion of the rigging and the bridge upon which the captain was standing. The bridge was ripped clean from the ship and the schooner, freeing itself from the steamer, carried the debris and the captain into the sea."

Punctured below the waterline, the Spanish steamer had been mortally wounded. "The water forced its way into the engine room, and, almost incredible to relate, came bursting out of the smokestack's mouth," explained Covas. "Two of the boats on the starboard side were carried away by the schooner's bowsprit. An attempt was made to lower the others, but there was not sufficient time to do so. One of them was lowered, but the tackle was not loosened in time, and before the boat could clear itself from the ship the steamer went down. The inmates of the boat were precipitated into the water. Some were carried down with the boat."

A passenger, Dr. Andres Jorge Valdes Rico, was in the smoking room talking with Señor Pedro when the ships collided. "They rushed on deck together and saw the bowsprint of the schooner towering above them and ripping away the rigging and deckhouses like chaff," reported the *New York Times*. "Señor Juan Pedro said, 'Are we lost?' and the doctor answered, 'if we are injured below the water line we are.' Just then Chief Engineer Francisco Serra came up from the engine room and announced that everything was gone below and the hull flooding rapidly. Even as they talked the vessel began to settle, and Mrs. Manuel Calvo, with her boy in her arms, came stumbling toward them, screaming, 'For God's sake, save my little one!' The engineer tried to get hold of the child, but the final tremble of the steamer came then, and he had just time to catch the fore rigging as she sank."

"The scene aboard the *Vizcaya* beggars description," said Covas. "At the shock of the collision the passengers and crew ran to the deck, then back again to their cabins to save their valuables. As for myself I did not think anything of saving my effects. When I reached the deck, Señor Deza, the supercargo, was at my side. He had charge of the ship's money. With it was much of his own. It was contained in a strong and heavy box. Seeing the condition of affairs he hastened below to secure the money. He appeared on deck with it. When the ship sank I found myself in the water. I espied Deza also struggling in the water with his treasure. He cried to me to save him. I asked him to throw away his gold. 'What good can it do you now? I said. 'Is not your life better than gold?' He replied that it was the Company's and the captain's money that he wanted to save. He struggled for a while in the water. I could not help him. He would not surrender his hold on the box. Its weight carried him to the bottom.

"I hastened to the stern of the ship," continued Covas, "and when I saw that it was going down I flung myself into the sea. When the vessel sank I swam to one of the masts and clung to it until rescued. I was half submerged in the water during the entire time, but I was able to retain my hold. Cold as the water was it was preferable to the air, which was bitter cold."

First Mate Perring laid the blame for the collision squarely on the *Vizcaya*. He told the *New York Tribune*, "At that time I had no idea we would sink, and ran forward and cried out to the people on the steamer's deck to find out what her name was, for I wanted to be able to hold somebody responsible for the damage done us. When we fell off, and laid alongside the steamer, her crew began to pour down on our decks. From the rate at which they dropped down on our deck I think there must have been thirty or forty of them there inside of a few minutes. I ran aft and told one of the men to clear away the boats. Then I let go the top most halyards. The captain called out to haul in the spanker, and in this work the Spaniards helped us. At this time I was afraid that the Spaniards would crowd into our boats and leave us to drown, so I told Mate Walker to stand by them and keep the Spaniards off.

"The confusion was very great at this time," Perring said, " and the Spaniards were running up and down the deck in deadly terror. . . . I began to feel the schooner settling at the bow and then I knew she was sinking. I said to the captain: 'Captain John, we have got to take to the boats.' He assented and seven of our men, including the captain and myself and four of the Spaniards, got into the small boat. When we got away a short distance two Spaniards sprang into the water and the men in the small boat picked them up. From the time we struck the steamer until we sank, was, I should judge, about fifteen minutes."

About forty *Vizcaya* crewmen saved themselves by climbing into the steamer's rigging. Three others climbed the masts of the *Cornelius Hargraves*. Chief Officer Felipo Hazas, who had climbed the rigging, told the *New York Times*, "The cold and wet were almost unbearable." Described as a tall, slight Spaniard with a sparse, dark beard, Hazas said he had never experienced a "night so long." One by one the crewmen lost their will to survive, dropping into the ocean to drown. By daylight only twelve still clung to their perches in the masts. A handful of passengers and crew found temporary refuge amid the wreckage floating in the calm waters. Over the next few hours, they surrendered one by one to the body-numbing cold water. All died.

Captain Allen and twelve other survivors in the ship's longboat rowed toward Barnegat Light. When they reached the surf they shouted "at the top of their lungs" in the hopes of attracting the attention of anyone on shore. Failing in this, they rowed back into the busy sea-lanes, hailed two passing steamers without success, and were finally rescued by a schooner after midnight.

Left behind on the *Cornelius Hargraves*, Mate Walker grasped a large gangplank and jumped overboard with it. He said in the *Tribune*, "As soon as I rose to the surface I got hold of the plank, to which thirteen of the Spanish vessel's men were clinging," Walker told a reporter. "The sea was not rough, but there was a heavy, long swell. All of a sudden a big wave washed us all off the plank. When I got back to it again there were seven of us left. Another wave carried off two men. One by one my comrades slipped off and disappeared. By 9 o'clock I was alone upon the plank. The moon shone brightly, but it was freezing cold and I had to battle with myself all the time to keep from giving up and going down. About 4 o'clock Friday morning I came up to a Spaniard who had a better raft than mine, who had been swept off the gang-plank. I then swam to him and we were picked up by the pilot boat *Marshall* at about 7 o'clock."

While afloat on his raft, Walker told the *Tribune*, a coop with two squawking ducks inside came drifting by. Taking hold of the coop, Walker managed to tie the ducks to his suspenders, thinking that even if he were swept out to sea he would not be hungry as long as he held on to the fowl. A big wave carried away both the ducks and his suspenders.

As dawn was breaking, the steamer *Humboldt*, nearing the end of its journey from Rio de Janeiro to New York City, came upon the scene of the disaster. The ship's chief steward, Charles Winham, told the *Tribune* that the *Humboldt*'s pilot was the first to spy the wreckage, calling out that he could see a steamer "straight ahead to the northwest" which appeared to be sinking. Summoned to the bridge, the captain gave orders to clear away the lifeboat as quickly as possible. "I went into the forerigging and could just make out some masts and sails in the distance. They seemed to come up out of the water. We steamed on at full speed and pretty soon I could make out the rig of a four-masted schooner with all sails set and the water over her deck. About 500 yards to the westward were the bare poles of a steamer. The steamer seemed to be sunk half way up to her mainyards.

"When we were within a mile of the vessels," continued Winham, "the captain ordered the speed slackened and the lead was hove several times as we approached the wrecks for fear of a sand bar, as we at first supposed both vessels had grounded. As it grew lighter I could make out a number of men in the steamer's rigging, but I could see no one on the schooner on account of the sails. There was no signal of distress flying from either vessel, but before we slowed up I saw one of the men waving what looked like a white shirt. The steamer stopped her screw about 100 yards from the wrecked steamer, and by that time it was light enough to make out both vessels very distinctly. I counted 10 men in the steamer's rigging and two in the foretop of the schooner."

The first officer and five men scrambled into the *Humboldt*'s lifeboat. "They pulled away to the steamer and made fast to the rigging of the mainmast, as her hull was entirely under water. They had a good deal of trouble in getting the men into the boat, however, as they seemed nearly frozen and shivering so that they could hardly help themselves. Most of them were dressed as if they had turned in and some of them had nothing on but a shirt. One poor fellow came near drowning as it was. In trying to cross over from the port to the starboard railing, he lost his hold and fell into the water. He was pulled into the lifeboat by one of the men in the stern sheets, who reached him an oar." The *Humboldt*'s seamen took off ten men from the steamer and two from the schooner's rigging. "We hailed the appearance of the *Humboldt*'s boats," said Chief Officer Hazas, "as only men who had looked on death twelve miserable hours could hail their savior."

When the boat returned with the survivors, Winham could see they were "nearly frozen." "They tumbled over the rail and were so weak they could scarcely stand. Their teeth chattered as if they would fall out. One fellow with bare legs, who wore a little silver cross suspended from his neck, fell on his knees and tried to thank God for his deliverance, but he was so benumbed he could only mumble."

Winham said that once the survivors had been taken below to warm themselves by the cabin fire, the *Humboldt*'s men questioned them about the accident. "They were all Spaniards and none of them could speak more than a few words of English. We were able to understand, however, that the captain and all of the passengers had gone down with the steamer when the collision occurred. It had all happened so quickly that only those who were on deck had been able to save themselves by springing into the rigging after a hurried attempt to clear away one of the boats.

"They all seemed unwilling to talk about the collision, even when questioned by the second officer, Mr. James, who speaks Spanish. The most they would say was that the schooner was entirely to blame for the accident, as the steamer had steered to port and given the schooner plenty of sea room had she not chosen to tack and try to run across the steamer's bows. Just how the collision happened we were unable to learn, and it certainly seems mysterious."

Picked up by the schooner *Sarah L. Davis*, Captain Allen and his crew reached Philadelphia on November 3. Described by the *Times* as "a hale, healthy man of rugged build, but of gentlemanly manner," Allen laid the blame for the collision squarely on the *Vizcaya*. "The collision was one of those things for which there was no reason and can be no excuse," Allen said to the *Times*. "The *Hargraves* was undoubtedly upon her own course, with the right of way assured to her. It was not her place to get out of the way of the steamer. It was the steamer's duty to keep out of our way, and this is what she failed to do. She either did not or would not see us, and the crash was the result. I suspect that the officer of the watch, instead of being upon the bridge when our lights and flare were seen by the watch, was at dinner, and it was only our whistle that called him and the Captain to their posts, but too late to avoid the collision."

With the *Vizcaya*'s third officer and captain dead, what happened on the steamer in the minutes just before the two ships collided will never be known. To the *New York Times* it was "evident that the disaster was one that could have been avoided with a little more care on the part of somebody. As a sailing vessel, the schooner *Cornelius Hargraves* had the right of way, but from all that can be learned, her officers saw the approaching steamer while yet a long way off, and a slight change of course would have prevented the fatality." The *Times* also questioned why the *Vizcaya* stayed its course as well. "Nothing existed to have obstructed the view of the third officer of the *Vizcaya*, Francisco Morillas, who had charge of the bridge, and whose duty it was to have so steered his vessel as to avoid the approaching schooner." Others wondered why Captain Allen had failed to make at least some rudimentary effort to rescue additional survivors, many of them desperately trying to stay afloat amid the wreckage.

The venerable rules of the sea are clear: Although powered ships must give way to sailing ships, no one in command of a vessel may assume "a right of way" up to the point of collision. Said the *Tribune:* "It is thought that both captains were reckless, and that either could have avoided the collision by giving way . . . three minutes before the collision occurred." The *New York Herald*, however, did not equivocate, blaming the collision and loss of life on what it called "the criminal carelessness of a down East skipper who drove a great four-masted coal laden schooner through the evening waters with all sail on."

Delaware—Barnegat Bay—July 8, 1898

Eight years after the *Vizcaya* and *Cornelius Hargraves* collided and sank, another steamer bound for southern ports also met disaster in the busy sea-lanes opposite Barnegat Light. This time a combination of very good luck and outstanding leadership saved the lives of all those aboard.

The Clyde Lines steamer *Delaware*, with a length of 250 feet and a beam of 37 feet, was only slightly smaller than the *Vizcaya*. Like the *Vizcaya*, it was powered by a combination of sails and conventional steam engine. Unlike the Spanish ship, however, the wooden-hulled *Delaware* had been built as a freighter with limited passenger accommodations. Launched in 1880, the three-decker had seen much hard service in the West Indies trade; when the U.S. government chartered many of the Clyde Line's best passenger ships to transport soldiers to Cuba and Puerto Rico during the Spanish-American War, the old *Delaware* was hastily refurbished and pressed into service on the line's New York, Charleston, and Florida route.

Figure 17. The *Delaware* burned until the morning after the fire began, eventually sinking close to the Manasquan Inlet. Divers who visit the site still recover debris from the wreck, including the ship's bell as late as 1989. From the *New York Herald*, July 10, 1898.

The ship's captain was Andrew D. Ingram, at thirty-five the youngest in the Clyde Line. Born to a seafaring family (his father was also a Clyde Line captain who had served in the Civil War), Ingram was at the beginning of an memorable career that would see him as the captain of the *Pawnee*, a freighter that caught fire and sank off Wilmington, North Carolina, in 1899, with all hands saved, and the victim of a deranged passenger who shot and wounded him in the abdomen as he captained the steamer *Mohawk* off the Carolinas in 1914. All that was ahead of Ingram, however, as he guided the *Delaware* from its East River pier, under the Brooklyn Bridge and out of New York Harbor on the afternoon of July 8, 1898. Entrusted to him was the safety of a crew of thirty-four, thirty-three passengers, including four children, and a cargo of "groceries, provisions, and dry goods" valued at $125,000 earmarked for the U.S. Army. The ship was worth about as much as its cargo. The *Delaware* passed carefully through the wartime mine fields off Sandy Hook during the late afternoon. Clear skies and calm seas delighted the passengers, who stood at the rails, admiring the harbor and the Twin Lights as the steamer headed south. Its destination was Jacksonville, with an intermediate stop at Charleston.

After dinner at seven, most of the passengers returned to their cabins and were asleep by nine. A few men lingered on deck, smoking cigars and enjoying the cool sea breezes. "All then was silent save the panting of the engine and the turning of the shaft and the rolling of the swash from off the bows."

"The voyage was without incident," reported the *New York Herald*, "and all went well until about nine o'clock that night, when one of the saloon stewards, who was on watch, smelled smoke, and promptly reported to Captain Ingram, who was on the bridge." The captain and first officer traced the source of the smoke to a small fire in the hold. A sailor sent below reported that some cargo was on fire but that the hold was so filled with freight and smoke that he was unable to pinpoint the fire's location, except that it was toward the ship's stern.

One of the first passengers to realize the ship was on fire was I. P. Ward, a railroad man from Augusta, Georgia. "I was sitting on the upper deck enjoying the cool breeze when my attention was caught by the sight of a thin column of smoke curling upward from the lower deck," Ward told the *New York Times*. "It was then about 10 o'clock. Though the hour was early, nearly everybody had retired. But there was one man sitting near me, and I called his attention to the smoke. It seemed very strange, and together we started to make an inspection. A deck hand passed us just then, and I asked what the cause of it was. He told me there was a fire in the hold. Almost at the same instant several sailors bearing axes appeared on the deck below and began chopping a hole through it."

After smashing their way through the deck, crewmen unreeled the after-deck hoses and tried to smother the fire by flooding the cargo hold with water. When the deck became too hot to stand on, the crew retreated to the saloon, rolled up the carpet and cut access holes there as well. As soon as the hold was breached, however, "smoke came through in such overpowering masses that it was deemed time to notify the passengers and prepare for the worst." It was then that Ingram gave two orders that undoubtedly saved passengers and crew: The first was to alter the ship's course for the New Jersey shore, then less than ten miles distant; the second was to instruct crew members not fighting the fire to make ready the ship's four boats for immediate lowering. Ordinarily shut down in the summer months, when their crews were working other jobs, the Jersey lifesaving stations were fully manned and operational because of the war with Spain. Ingram hoped that the burning ship would be sighted and rescue boats launched. By running the ship toward the shore, calculated Ingram, wind currents would retard the advancing flames, preventing them from enveloping the entire vessel before help arrived. Crewmen began firing rockets to attract the attention of any ships in the area.

Captain Ingram sent First Officer Macbeth and the stewardess, Ella Hill, below to rouse the sleeping passengers. "I was in my stateroom when one of the officers rapped on my door, and in a perfectly calm tone told me not to be alarmed, but to get up quietly and dress, as something had happened," P. N. Simons of Charleston told the *Herald*'s reporter. "When I asked him what it was, he said that a fire had been discovered in the hold, but that there was no immediate danger. The captain desired all passengers to get on deck as soon as possible. He added that I would not be permitted to take any hand baggage with me. Then I heard him go to the next stateroom and repeat the instructions. He did it all as calmly as if he had been summoning us to dinner."

By this time, flames had broken through the deck and heavy smoke began seeping into many of the cabins. "The passengers evidently understood the emergency of the summons," continued Ward. "They flung open their stateroom doors, and thronged into the hallway. Yet there was no excitement, only the confusion of hurry. One man cracked his door, and thrusting his head out, asked what the trouble was. I told him I thought the ship was one fire. 'Oh, is that all!' he said, and he closed the door again. Later, I saw him on the upper deck, fully dressed and smoking a pipe.

"The male passengers turned their attention to the women, and assisted them up the steps," explained Ward. "When I got back to the deck nearly everybody was grouped forward watching the flames, which were then burning fiercely. I rushed back down to get my grip, in which was a gold watch, a diamond bracelet, and a set of diamond studs I had just bought, but the passage had become filled with smoke, and I found it impossible to reach my stateroom. I again went on deck. With me were two or three men who had evidently gone below, like myself, to secure their baggage. When we reached the deck for the last time the boats were swinging clear, and the women and children being handed in."

Captain Ingram addressed the assembled passengers: "It would be necessary to abandon the ship," he said, "but we were in no danger, as there were plenty of boats and the shore was in plain view." Women and children would leave first.

"Of course the women and children were much frightened," passenger Simons told the *Herald*, " but they all behaved splendidly, which was greatly due to the brave conduct of the stewardess. I tell you, that women is a 'brick.' It was wonderful how the trained crew managed to get the first boat launched. The women and children were all in front and the sailors bundled them up in blankets and stowed them in the boat until it was full, when they cast off and stood by. Life preservers were served out to all of us, and we were shown how to adjust them properly." An officer and two crewmen were put in charge of each boat as it was lowered into the ocean.

Not everyone obeyed orders. Several male passengers who attempted to climb into the boats reserved for women were unceremoniously tossed back onto the deck. "When my turn came to get in a boat," remembered Ward, "a fellow dragging a trunk passed me and flung the trunk into the little craft. Four men who were already seated calmly, and of one accord, picked it up and tossed it overboard."

"After the first two boats got away the fire spread rapidly, sweeping forward along the decks and threatening to envelope the whole ship," reported the *Herald*. "In spite of this, however, there was not the slightest relaxation of discipline, and the seamen worked manfully in their efforts to launch the two starboard boats, in spite of the flames playing all around them." It was at this point that one of the seamen, named Lubline, was severely burned about the face, hands, chest, and back when "an outburst of flame" caught him and several others in its grasp. Despite the injuries, the crew managed to launch the remaining two boats. The discipline of the crew was remarkable. "Even when the boats were lowered the men stood by, not attempting to enter them until they were ordered to do so by the captain. When the boats finally pushed off there remained on the blazing deck only Captain Ingram and six of his officers and men."

Ingram and his remaining men, cut off from the boats by the spreading flames, rushed to the ship's bow. "Every man was animated by the captain's example, and when he called on them to hustle about and get together material for a raft, they fell to work with a will. Two wooden hatch gratings lashed together with loose spars served for one raft, but it was not big enough for all, and after it had been thrown overboard, the brave fellows hung back when the captain ordered them to lower themselves over the side. Finally three of them obeyed orders, loading the frail craft to its full capacity. When they had pushed off the captain and the rest found two more gratings and lashed them together and again launched the raft, on which three men lowered themselves, leaving the captain standing on the forecastle." Captain Ingram stood there for a minute, then swung over the side, lowered himself to the raft, cut the rope, and pushed off with his crewmen.

Two of the boats took the rafts in tow and pulled them away from the burning hulk. It was then 11:20 P.M., recalled Chief Engineer Platt, who remembered to look at his watch. "The *Delaware* was then almost a mass of fire, the flames having swept up the rigging, ignited the deckhouses around which they licked viciously, and even wrapped themselves around the masts." Ingram ordered the boats to keep together and stay clear of the shore where they might capsize in the surf.

"While the boats lay tossing and heaving the passengers kept up their courage by singing songs, in which the women and children joined. The boats lay within a quarter of a mile of the blazing steamer, which was soon on fire from stem to stern. . . . In about half an hour a terrific explosion occurred, hurling a volcano of blazing fragments 100 feet into the air. This was followed by a series of minor explosions." Some of the passengers claimed that ammunition aboard the ship destined for the army had exploded, an allegation the Clyde Line would later vehemently deny.

The boats had been in the water less than an hour when a white surfboat rowed by oarsmen was seen rapidly approaching from the shore. The lifesaving boat from the Cedar Creek station had barely arrived when the fishing vessel *S. B. Miller* hove into sight, joining the flotilla of boats and rafts. While the passengers and crew were being transferred to the fishing boat, the seagoing tug *Ocean King* arrived on the scene, took all on board (save Captain Ingram and several crew members) and set a course back to New York.

Ingram refused to go aboard the tug, declaring, according to the *Herald*, "that it was his duty to stand by his ship as long as there was any hope of saving anything." The captain remained in the lifesaving boat until daybreak. When it was evident the *Delaware*, by then a gutted, smoldering wreck, was beyond saving, he was rowed to the Cedar Creek station, took a train to New York, and there received a hero's welcome from his passengers, crew, and Clyde Line officials. What was left of the *Delaware* sank near the Manasquan Inlet.

"No more splendid example of discipline and courage is on record than that displayed by the crew of the Clyde line steamship *Delaware*," wrote the *Herald*. "Absolute order was maintained on the American ship from the moment when the fire was discovered until the Captain, having seen the last of the passengers and crew safe in the boats, lowered himself over the side." Captain Ingram, reported the press, was "totally exhausted" by his ordeal. "All he would say was that he had simply done his duty, but spoke in terms of pardonable pride of the splendid discipline of his crew." Clyde Line agents interviewed by the *Herald* called Ingram "one of the best men that have ever been in its service."

I. P. Ward, the Georgia railroad man who was among the first passengers to notice that the ship was on fire, had other thoughts on his mind as he bought new clothing at the Clyde Line's expense. "Tomorrow I'm going to make a new start for home," he told a reporter. "And I am going to make it by rail."

CHAPTER 5

NATURAL DISASTERS

Those who suffered through 2011's Hurricane Irene, followed by that year's Halloween snowstorm, and then Hurricane Sandy in 2012 might disagree with the experts who claim that New Jersey's weather is usually benign. Yet despite the recent brutal storms, exceptional events—hurricanes, tornados, blizzards, and heat waves—are rare. Located in the middle latitudes of North America, with three thousand miles of dry land to the west and three thousand miles of ocean to the east, the cold of Canada to the north, and the warmth of the tropics to the south, the state enjoys a favored position on the globe. Seldom does nature turn deadly.

Severe winter storms can cause economic disruption, injury, and even death. Cleanup costs have always been enormous. The ice storm of January 5, 1873, was the most damaging of the nineteenth century. Countless branches snapped, thousands of trees were uprooted, and in all the large cities telegraph poles and wires, coated with a heavy layer of ice, fell down, making travel virtually impossible for several days. On February 11–14, 1899, a blizzard struck New Jersey, dropping more than thirty-one inches of snow, the greatest of any single period on record. This followed by one day the coldest morning in the state's history, when the mercury dropped below zero in all twenty-one counties.

The Blizzard of '88—March 11–14, 1888

The twenty or so inches of snow that fell on March 11–14, 1888, would have
gone into the record books as just another forgettable late winter storm
had not its gale-force winds and subfreezing temperatures transformed
it into what we remember still today as the Blizzard of '88. By the time it
ended, the storm that paralyzed much of the northeastern United States
for five days left behind upward of $20 million in property damage and
economic loss and, according to some estimates, claimed nearly four hundred lives. Despite the passage of time, it remains the benchmark against
which severe winter storms are measured.

In New Jersey, the storm was felt in all twenty-one counties: snowfall
ranged from twenty-five inches in Union County to ten inches along the
lower Delaware River; winds were clocked at 60 miles per hour during the
storm's height. After it was over, state residents were too busy clearing away
the great mounds of snow to tally New Jersey's losses. Contemporary newspaper accounts, however, leave no doubt that the damage toll was significant. Three days after the snowfall ended, search parties in Jersey City still
busy looking for frozen bodies in the snowdrifts found the remains of John
Short buried under a snow bank near Scheutzen Park; five residents missing
since Monday had not been located and were presumed dead. At least eight
people in Newark had perished, among them James Murphy, an escaped
City Hospital inmate who was found trapped in the snow on Bank Street
clad only in his nightshirt, and a man known simply as the Crazy Fisherman,
discovered in a drift near the Third Police Precinct. Train wrecks caused by
the drifting snow claimed additional lives. As the snow gradually melted,
more bodies were discovered. The greatest loss of life occurred off the coast
of New Jersey, where an estimated forty people drowned. After the storm,
thirteen vessels were found abandoned at sea; half could not be identified.
Another thirteen had been blown against the shore near Sandy Hook, most
of them sunk or badly damaged. All in all, said the *Newark Sunday Call*, it
was "the greatest blizzard known east of the Allegheny Mountains."

Figure 18. Drawing of four Pennsylvania Railroad locomotives straining to clear the tracks between Newark and Jersey City. From the *New York Daily Graphic*, March 15, 1888.

The Blizzard of '88 caught New Jersey entirely by surprise. The winter had been the mildest in years. Spring was in the air as March began. Saturday, March 10, dawned clear and pleasant. The weather forecast for Sunday, March 11, was "cloudy followed by light rain." New Jerseyans who woke early on Sunday to prepare for church were greeted instead by an unexpected storm. "After night-fall on [Saturday] a gale of wind sprang up which lasted through the night," wrote the *Madison Weekly Eagle*, its report typical of conditions throughout the state. The windstorm "was followed by a heavy rain which continued from about 10 o'clock on Sunday morning, until about the same hour at night, when the rain changed to hail, which after a short time turned to snow; as the snow fell the wind seemed to increase in power, and drove the snow, which was very fine, through every crack and crevice." Monday morning, the 12th, dawned with the wind and snow on the increase, a wind, continued the *Eagle*, that "seemed to blow from every quarter on the compass at once, driving the snow before it, thus causing buildings even a few feet away to be obscured from sight, and catching up the snow when it reached the ground, forming it into mounds and causing drifts that made locomotion almost impossible.

The snow and wind continued without intermission during the day and night, with the only change that the power of the wind at night seemed to increase." Throughout Tuesday, the 13th, "the same conditions prevailed, until when night fell upon the scene the snow had ceased, though the wind continued to blow in fearful gusts." On Wednesday, the storm's fourth day, scattered light snow persisted across the state. The winds remained brisk, piling the fallen snow in ever-higher drifts.

Bitterly cold temperatures, heavy drifting snow, and gale-force winds define a blizzard. On Tuesday, the 13th, the state experienced its coldest temperature when the mercury dropped to one degree below zero in Newton. Elsewhere temperatures hovered in the teens and twenties during the day, dipping lower at night. The Raritan River was frozen solid from Perth Amboy to New Brunswick. Immense ice flows clogged the Hudson River.

The howling winds blew the snow into colossal drifts: In Newton, a thirty-foot-high drift obscured the Presbyterian Church; ten- to fifteen-foot drifts were common elsewhere. In Newark, according to reports, houses were buried so deeply that only their chimneys were visible. Commonly, in the cities one side of a street would be blown clear of snow while the other would be invisible under drifts that reached to the second story of buildings.

The winds were at their fiercest along the Jersey Shore. Atlantic City newspapers said the storm was the worst since the city's settlement. Beginning at 3:00 A.M. Monday morning with a fierce hailstorm followed by a heavy fall of snow and 60-mile-per-hour winds, the blizzard shut the city down tight for nearly three days. At Cape May, Monday's high winds first ripped off the roof of the Burlington Thread Mill and then collapsed its walls, destroying the building and injuring several workers. It was, said the *Cape May Gazette*, "one of the most terrific snow and wind storms that has ever occurred in this vicinity. The air was thick with snow, and frame buildings were groaning and trembling as if they were ready to fly apart. Few people slept." Near West Cape May, the Knickerbocker Ice House was blown down, houses knocked over, trees uprooted, and the Electric Light Company's smokestack toppled. In Sea Isle City, houses were unroofed, chimneys shattered, and outbuildings ripped apart.

During the worst of the blizzard, not one vessel dared enter or leave the port of New York. At sea, the winds reached 100 miles per hour. The *Starbuck*, a pilot boat, was cruising off Barnegat when the *Japanese*, a British fruit steamer, struck it. A second wave tossed the two vessels together again, tearing off the pilot boat's main rigging and tossing four sailors into the raging waters where they drowned. The yacht *Cythera*, with a crew of eight, sank with all aboard lost.

The full gale that blew most of March 12 and 13 left Camden "in a serious condition," reported the *Philadelphia Inquirer*. Because the city's water supply could not be replenished, reported the paper, officials feared that if any fires broke out, they could not be extinguished. Scores of businesses, including the city's newspaper, had to suspend activity when water needed to operate steam-powered machinery began to run low. The failure of the water supply was blamed on the high northwest winds, which the paper said literally blew the river into the bay, making it impossible to pump water from the Delaware River into the municipal system. Railroads improvised, using tugs to pump river water into locomotive boilers. The ferries *Arctic* and *Baltic*, which usually carried thousands of commuters daily between Camden and Philadelphia, were stuck on the bar opposite Cooper's Point because of the low water in the river. The early afternoon tide, according to river men, was one of the lowest ever seen, exposing the mud bars between New Jersey and Pennsylvania for the first time in memory.

After impenetrable drifts near Bordentown blocked the main line of the Camden and Amboy division of the Pennsylvania Railroad, Camden's only rail link was with Philadelphia. When a train bound for Haddonfield became stuck in a huge drift near Starr's Crossing, its passengers were forced to spend a miserable night huddled around the cars' stoves. Telegraph and telephone poles lay on the ground everywhere, while nearly every street was

Figure 19. The Blizzard of 1888 shut down much of the Northeast for nearly five days. In this photo, a group of Newark factory workers are about to spread of load of gravel on an almost impassable street. Courtesy of the Newark Public Library.

blocked by downed trees, many of them torn up by their roots. Countless sheds and barns in Camden were blown down by the gale-force winds.

In an era when to lose a day's work was to lose a day's pay, many woke up Monday morning determined to go to work regardless of the nasty weather. Despite the swirling snow, tens of thousands of bankers, merchants, shop-keepers, and factory and office workers set out that morning, fully expecting the trolleys and trains to be waiting at the station, ready to take them to their destination. Nineteenth-century weather forecasts were at best vague; only those who read Sunday's newspaper knew that a storm was at hand. None realized that they faced a blizzard of historic proportion.

Typical was the experience of a reporter for Jersey City's *Evening Journal*, who awoke early Monday morning, left his home at 8:00 A.M., and, as he reported in that evening's newspaper, was soon "floundering in a six foot deep snow drift." Plunging ahead with his umbrella, "which had instantly been turned inside out" by the howling winds, he found "the town another place. Nothing of life was to be seen. Houses seemed empty and desolate, and the snow piled high against their doors was untrodden by the foot of man. In places the drifts were many feet high. The very atmosphere seemed made of white particles, which stung and cut the face like sharp needles. Every breath was drawn with difficulty and was charged with minute ice particles." Down Ivy Place the *Journal* reporter trudged. "On the north side of that street the snow was piled up to the second story windows, and no sign of life was to be seen. On the south side, along Library Hall, the walk was clear, and down the sharp incline the luckless tramp was blown. On Grand street there was the sign of a road. Some powerful engine had forced a path through the heavy drifts, but no sign of a car track was visible." No trolleys were running. "It was plain that those who would reach old Jersey City must walk."

Trudging along through the snow, the *Journal*'s reporter heard a cry for help. After searching for several minutes he found a woman trapped in a drift. "She had been blown off the street into the meadows. She was with difficulty rescued and was left in the lee of a building, gasping for breath. A little further along a huge truck was standing in the roadway. It had been abandoned evidently hours before. Stranded wagons were met with at frequent intervals along Grand street.

"A short distance below Woodward street, a letter carrier was found stranded. He was hugging the lee of a building and cursed the inexorable law that compelled him to make a pretense at least of doing duty. A few steps further on a [trolley] car was met, stalled in the drifts. It was the only one the writer saw on any road all the way down. As the route reached the open meadow district the traveling grew more difficult. The road was strewn with telephone wires, and others were switching about in the wind, to the peril of all passersby."

When the reporter reached downtown Jersey City, he found conditions no better. "Abandoned trucks were seen at frequent intervals, the houses appeared to be scaled by the snowdrifts, business was at a standstill, and the town seemed to be deserted. On the way down the hill side half a dozen milk wagons were found abandoned by the drivers. The milk in the cans was frozen solid, the harness piled in a heap on the front of the wagons, and everything showed that the driver had jumped on the horses and gone home in haste. Down near Warren street an enterprising shopkeeper was shoveling off snow, and a doctor on foot rubbed his hands and shouted, 'This is the weather to make pneumonia.'"

A *New York Herald* newsman who spent the weekend in Caldwell woke up Monday morning "astonished," he wrote, "to find that a genuine old fashioned white coverlid had fallen on the earth's bosom; that it lay three or four feet deep on the level, and that the fierce wind with snarling buffetings was building it up mountains high wherever it could have its way. All around for miles and miles fences were almost obliterated, houses were clothed in heavy capes of ermine that hung over their eaves in deep fringes and the woods looked as if they had adorned themselves for the occasion in quaint, old, fairy made lace, for, though the wind was insolently violent, the particles of snow or sleet were very moist and readily adhered to objects on which they alighted."

To reach New York City, the reporter usually took a stagecoach from Caldwell to Montclair and then another to Newark, where he caught an eastbound train. When he reached the coach stop at eight thirty in the morning, the drifts were already so high that the regular stagecoach could not budge. "A large open sleigh was then brought out, with a pair of giant horses, and a driver who proved to be good humored in spite of his occasional incivility.

"Words cannot begin to describe that ride . . . ," wrote the reporter when he finally arrived at the *Herald* office. "How the wind blew! How it searched for one's marrow and having found it seemed to whistle through one's very bones! How the sharpened sleet drove into one's face and down

one's shivering back and up one's gaping coat sleeves! It was a treacher-
ous and bitter and stinging wind. Unless a close watch were kept it would
speedily freeze any portion of human flesh that was exposed to it." The
temperature, he reckoned, was about fifteen degrees above zero. "A gentleman from Caldwell soon discovered that his ears were frozen white and
stiff." When it departed Caldwell by way of Bloomfield Avenue there were
only four passengers in the stage. More were picked up in Verona and other
stops until twelve commuters, among them four women, huddled aboard.
"The spirit of jollity reigned in spite of the elements. Most of the time the
driver could not see ten yards in front of his horses and they sank into the
snow at nearly every step as high as their bellies. Toiling up the back range
of the first Orange range was a tedious process. The good steeds puffed
and sweated, but pulled steadily. There was no intermission in the hard
pelting of the storm, the spiteful lashings of the wind, the rapid accumula-
tion of the snow. No one had much hope of getting to the city, after all, for
the driver had given forth the dismal news just as he was starting that the
only train which had ventured down the road had found the cut at Glen
Ridge so full of snow that it could go no further.

"Going down the Orange range at a comparatively rapid pace, the
ride became positively exciting. The horses . . . dashed milky clouds of
spray around them . . . , and from their nostrils blew great clouds of steam
which congealed and turned into glittering drops almost as soon as it
met the withering gale. Ice decked the harness, the manes and the tails
of the animals. The driver and the fur that enveloped him, and the hair
and beards of the passengers were all encrusted with an icy fret work. The
sleigh sometimes tilted one way and sometimes the other. It ploughed up
over mountains of snow and down again into valleys." The sleigh reached
Montclair an hour after it left Caldwell.

Stagecoaches and sleighs in the winter were commonly used for travel
in the countryside. In the cities, horse-drawn streetcars (electric trolleys
were not introduced until two years after the storm) provided mass transportation; long-distance travel was by train. As the rain turned to snow on

Sunday evening, it dawned on the railroad and streetcar companies that a blizzard might be at hand. Unable to break through the drifts, the horse car lines gave up the ghost early Monday morning, unhitching their horses and leaving empty cars stuck in the snow. The railroad companies were likewise completely unprepared to cope with the storm's fury. None had snowplows, and many had neglected to keep their tracks clear by the usual expedient of running empty trains.

New Jersey commuters who boarded early morning trains had no idea of the obstacles ahead. "The train was crowded to its utmost holding," said the *New York Times* about the Jersey Central train that reached Jersey City at 9:30 A.M. on Monday. "Snow and sleet came through the smallest crevices. It was not more comfortable than a refrigerator." At Jersey City's Cortlandt Street slip, exhausted commuters boarded ferries for the trip to New York City, a journey they would long remember. "After a long delay the boat started to plow its way to New York," reported the *Times*, printing a graphic account about one ferry that departed Monday evening. "It got within a few hundred feet of the slip, when its momentum was stopped by the heavy ice floe and the engines were unable to force it through and into the slip. The pilot tried to land at the Baltimore & Ohio pier, but after battling with the ice for an hour and more the coal in the bunkers ran low and he put back to Jersey City for a fresh supply. He tried to reach New York several times, but without success. . . . There were about 200 people on the boat and they made things lively in an effort to keep warm, as the cabins were insufficiently heated and the cold blasts from the river penetrated the joints of the doors and set the shivers to skirmishing among them. When the boat returned to Jersey City the passengers left in a body and rushing into Taylor's Hotel took remedies for the cold." Another ferry, the *Communipaw*, bucked the turbulent Hudson until a crosscurrent nearly swept it out into the bay.

Conditions were no better in central Jersey. An immense drift fifteen feet deep about a mile from Princeton Junction blocked a train that departed Philadelphia for New York on Sunday night. "There the train was

obliged to stay from 10 o'clock Monday morning until 11 o'clock [Wednes-
day] morning, when a relief party succeeded in getting the hungry and
half-frozen passengers back to Trenton," said the *Philadelphia Inquirer*.
"The experiences of the travelers were fearful. During the two nights they
were obliged to walk up and down through the cars to keep from freezing.
The fires were kept burning in the stoves, but the wind blew so fiercely that
they did not warm the cars. Several of the men attempted to walk to Princeton Junction, a distance of a mile, and nearly perished in the drifts. They
returned to the trains with great difficulty.... Many of them when taken to
Trenton, had their ears and feet badly frozen." Passengers on the train were
without food until Tuesday morning when some enterprising locals who
tunneled through the drifts enveloping the cars sold sandwiches for the
"outrageous price" of fifty cents each. According to the paper, a relief party
took nearly twelve hours to reach the stranded passengers. A train powered by four engines failed to blast through the drifts. Stuck in the snow,
the passenger train had to be rescued by a fifth engine sent from Trenton.
The drifts in many places were twelve to fifteen feet deep.

The *New York Herald* reporter who traveled by sleigh from Caldwell to
Montclair climbed aboard a crowded Jersey City–bound train, grateful to
find a seat. "The train started about 10 o'clock and moved but slowly," he
continued, his experience typical of thousands of fellow commuters that
Monday morning. "After many halts, backings and fitful advances, it stuck
at length hopelessly at the curve of the Bloomfield branch, just west of
the junction with the main line at Roseville. Two, three, and four engines
were employed, but to no purpose. The drive wheels whirled around in the
snow, but could not get hold upon the rails. The forward coupling rods of
two locomotives were jerked out in tugging at the train. During the dead
wait of two hours that ensued many of the passengers got out and made
their way with great difficulty over to the Orange train, which was in sight.

"Meanwhile, foraging delegations had already exhausted all the prov-
ender that could be obtained at the station.... It was not a joyous crowd.
It was not a witty crowd. It was decidedly stupid and lugubrious.... In the

forenoon the cry had been 'On to Gotham!' In the afternoon it was 'Back to our homes!' Homesickness and a quasi seasickness were both present. The cars would rock from side to side like ships in a cross sea when the wind hurled itself against them with its demoniac force. Then you could see some of the weak brethren turn pale around the mouth."

The train back to Morristown was standing-room only. "After the locomotives had spluttered and fumed and whistled a good deal three cars were finally detached from this train and the other two were pulled on. Every moment that had elapsed, however, during the last six hours had added to the depth of the drifts. Every now and then the wheels of the locomotives would slip and whirl futilely about. The whistles would toot in vainly encouraging tones. Perhaps a quarter of a mile was made in an hour. The curtailed train had even reached the down grade which leads straight into Newark, yet the cars budged so little that they were fast being snowed in. At 3 o'clock the engines abandoned them, having exhausted both steam and fuel, and went into Newark nominally in search of these, but really to report the utter impossibility of moving the cars until the storm should cease."

As Monday wore on, the gale-force winds blew the falling snow into ever higher drifts. At Newark, within a half-mile of each other, three full Delaware and Lackawanna passenger trains sat on the rails, stalled in the deepening snow. "The only convenient refuge, other than the cars for those at the Roseville junction, was the station," continued the *Herald* reporter. "Those in the advance train had found a supply of sandwiches and liquors at a petty lager beer saloon, on Orange street, but this was small and offered no adequate accommodation for the night. The few lady passengers had timorously remained at the Roseville junction. But there seemed no hope of nightly shelter for any one, except in a walk into Newark. This was not to be lightly undertaken. Those who had gone out on foraging expeditions declared that to walk against the wind through the drifts for a mile or so was as much as a man's life was worth. Luckily the direction of the wind was toward Newark. All the chances of getting livery conveyances either way had been canvassed and declared hopeless. The hope of seeing home, wife and children that night was reluctantly given up."

By four in the afternoon it became apparent that no locomotives were coming to the rescue of the stranded commuters. "One by one the more resolute of the passengers buttoned and tied themselves up as tightly as they could and went forward. Some who incautiously stepped off the south side of the train instead of the north nearly disappeared forever, sinking in the snow up to their armpits.

"The temperature had steadily fallen all day. The foot journey into Newark—about a mile and a quarter, through the bitter tempest, was exhausting. A few townsfolk were staggering home against the wind, and they looked like strange, uncanny beings as they toiled toward us out of the blinding mist." According to the *Herald*'s reporter, at least 800 "snow stalled travelers" from the suburbs finally reached Newark on foot.

The story was the same all over New Jersey. A train that managed to leave Camden on Monday morning was blocked for more than thirty hours by a huge drift near Princeton. More than 250 passengers suffered as the wind-driven snow buried the coaches, baggage car, and two engines. Not until Tuesday morning did relief arrive, when students from nearby College of New Jersey (now Princeton University) reached the cars, carrying baskets of food. In Trenton, an estimated 250 stranded passengers spent Monday night huddled in the main station. Railroad traffic from Trenton south was at an absolute standstill. No trains moved on the Camden and Amboy division of the Pennsylvania Railroad. Twenty-three engines of the West Jersey Railroad were struck fast in drifts. Twelve trains were snowed under in Burlington County along with hundreds of passengers aboard. Asbury Park was without train service for eighty hours, with street-level tracks buried under nine feet of snow in some places. Further north, fourteen trains with more than 1,500 passengers aboard were stalled near South Orange, their progress halted when a freight train clearing the tracks ran into a snow bank and derailed. In Jersey City seven hundred men worked for more than six hours shoveling away a twenty-foot-high drift blocking the cut just east of Marion Station.

"At the Elizabethport Station over 100 men were huddled together like cattle all night Monday," said the *Elizabeth Journal*. "There was no place even to sit down. At the little station on the Newark branch road thirty-five people sought shelter from the furious storm which blew the shutters off the windows, smashed the glass and drifted the fine snow in through the broken crevices. The fire inside melted the snow and converted the floor into a pool of slush, ankle deep, in which the people had to stand. The shutters were picked up and utilized for seats."

At the New Point Hotel, proprietor Phillip Shouble provided free food and drink to the bosses and workingmen from the nearby Singer Sewing Machine factory. "Three men slept all night on top of his big icebox, while the others were strewn around on benches and chairs." Six hundred passengers were stranded in the Elizabeth station. "The trains that were fortunate enough to reach this city brought scores of passengers from all stations within 25 miles of the city, and the waiting rooms of the Union depot were yesterday packed from noon till night," said the Elizabeth paper. "The eating houses, wholly unprepared for such a rush of business, were nearly eaten out of provisions. But the worst difficulty was encountered in attempts to accommodate the storm stayed people for the night. The parlor cars on the road were utilized, the hotels were crowded, and not a few hospitable people opened their hearts and homes and accommodated many." Stranded passengers were put up in nearby Trinity Church, which opened its doors to hundreds unable to find any other place of refuge.

The Jersey City railroad station "looked like a gypsy camp," with passengers stranded in the waiting room for two days, among them the young ladies of the Lily Clay Gaiety Company who spent the night in an endless poker game. The game ended only when the chips—gumdrops from the station's candy stand—were all eaten. Also stranded in Jersey City were sixty-five members of the New York Casino Company. Their trip from Boston to Baltimore interrupted, they found accommodations for the night on the Pennsylvania Railroad's transfer boat docked on the Hudson River.

New Jersey's cities resembled ghost towns on Monday and Tuesday. Banks were closed, newspaper and mail delivery were suspended, the trains and streetcars stopped running, and fresh food grew scarce. Although some stores managed to open their doors, customers were few. The few clerks who managed to report for work stood around with little to do. Deliveries of milk, bread, and fresh meat were interrupted. Coal stocks were virtually exhausted. And in Jersey City, beer was running short. "Brewers' wagons were abandoned in every direction," reported the *Evening News*, tongue in cheek, "and since then no lager has been supplied to the saloons. This threatened famine affects the Fourth District seriously. The majority of its inhabitants can dispense with milk, but a scarcity of beer disarranges everything."

Most factories sent their workers home early on Monday. The Singer Sewing Machine works at Elizabethport employed 3,200 people. The 1,800 who made it to work on Monday stayed until noon, when factory managers decided to close because the coal supply used to heat the building began running low. Some women wisely refused to leave the plant and slept there Monday night. Many of the men decided to walk the quarter mile to the nearby railroad station, where they hoped to catch a train to Newark, leaving in groups of twenty or so for safety. P. Kenny Dilts, one of the men who walked to the station, told the *New York Herald* that the groups "meant to keep together, but the storm was so terrible that before we were half way we were hopelessly separated. As I went on I met other men who had gone before. Some were helpless. The face of one was a perfect glare of ice. His eyelids were frozen fast and he was groping blindly along, and as I came up he fell into a drift. I waded up to him, broke the ice from his eyes, and tried to rouse him. He was almost in a stupor. I beat him and cuffed him till he recovered sufficiently to struggle on toward the station. I helped four or five men in this way.

"At last by only superhuman efforts I reached the station," continued Dilts. "Six men I found had been terribly frozen on the way. They were all taken to the New Point Hotel. The hands of some of them, the ears of others and even portions of their bodies were frozen. A man named Sherwood had both of his hands frozen to the wrists. Behind me, as I afterward learned, a man named Ellis was picked up out of the snow stiff and breathless. He was carried to the station and died soon afterward. Two other men were missing from our party. I do not doubt they are buried in the drifts." Some three hundred men from New York, Newark, and towns nearby crowded the station. "All were so exhausted and cowed by their dreadful walk that, though they were very anxious to get to Elizabeth, only twelve dared make the attempt to reach that city," explained Dilts. "It was three and a half miles distant, and it was a hard struggle, though not to be compared to the awful quarter of a mile in the teeth of the fierce gale which blew into our faces on the walk from the works to the station. The wind blew so fearfully that it was almost impossible to breathe, and this and the sleet that dashed into our faces and froze there bewildered and blinded us, and was the cause of the awful suffering which many experienced." Much the worse for wear, Dilts reached Newark on Tuesday morning.

Laborers Charles Lee, age eighteen; James Marshall, age seventeen; and Alexander Bennett, foreman of the nickel plating department at the Singer plant, took another route, leaving on Monday for their homes on Staten Island in a small boat, something they had done every day for years. When the men failed to return to work on Wednesday a search party went out looking for them. According to the *Newark Evening News*, after several hours the searchers found Bennett and Lee lying "frozen stiff" alongside a haystack in the Staten Island meadows four miles from where they had landed. Marshall, who had crawled into the haystack, was barely able to call for help when he saw his rescuers. "His hands and feet were terribly frozen." Carried to a farmhouse "delirious and in terrible agony," Marshall said the three men had wandered about for hours in the blinding snow until they found the haystack. Barely conscious, his friends soon died of

exposure. On Friday the newspapers reported that Marshall, his frostbitten hands and feet amputated, had also died.

Similar stories were repeated everywhere. At noon on Monday, John
Weller began walking home from his job at New Brunswick's New Jersey
Rubber Factory. At five-thirty that evening, two passersby saw "a tin can, a
pair of gloves and the top of the head of a person sticking out of a snowbank." It was Weller, "completely exhausted and suffering greatly from
the cold." According to the story in the *New Brunswick Times*, neighbors
took him to a nearby store, plied him with "stimulants," gave him supper
and plenty of coffee and put him to bed. In Newark a man on his way to
work fell into a sewer. When he was found, his hands were frozen to the
iron grating. After waiting all night aboard their stranded train at South
Orange, two exasperated stockbrokers from Summit organized fellow passengers into two groups that agreed to walk back to Summit, a six-mile
journey. Although both groups made it home, three men nearly perished
from exhaustion and exposure and others suffered from frostbitten ears,
noses, toes, and fingers.

Figure 20. On Monday, March 12, 1888, five Lehigh Valley locomotives heading west on a rescue mission derailed at Musky Bridge near Hackettstown,
injuring seven railroad workers and killing the lead engineer, who was
crushed and scalded to death. Courtesy of Thomas T. Tabor.

John Henriman of Milltown set out through the snow toward Raritan on Monday evening to fetch a doctor for his sick wife. Losing his way in the blinding snow, Henriman froze to death. When concerned neighbors forced their way into his home, they found the wife dead and her children on the verge of starvation.

The blizzard conditions that prevailed on Monday and Tuesday played havoc with the state's railroads. The number of wrecks and loss of life, though never tallied, was considerable. All of the state's rail lines suffered the loss of engines and rolling stock; at least a dozen employees were injured or killed. A Jersey Central local, running wildcat from station to station picking up passengers, collided with the rear of a stalled train. Later, a Jersey Central snowplow crashed into another train while trying to force its way through a drift; three people were killed and six others injured. On the Lehigh Valley line, a brakeman who jumped off his train to flag down an approaching train simply disappeared into a snowbank and was never seen again. Near Stanhope, three engines tumbled down an embankment, killing one of the engineers and badly scalding two others. A cattle train overturned near Washington in Warren County while trying to plow through an enormous drift. It took until Thursday for a crew of railway workers to jack a train that jumped the rails near Manasquan back onto the tracks.

On Monday morning, the 6:20 out of Bound Brook was struggling to make its way through the drifts when a New York freight following on the track cleared by the passenger train crashed into it, telescoping two coaches. Although no passengers were seriously hurt, the conductor and brakeman were badly injured. Hauling two wrecking cars crowded with one hundred workers, four engines were sent out Wednesday morning from Easton to open the Lehigh Valley railroad. After successfully plowing through countless drifts, the engines encountered a mound of hard-packed snow below Three Bridges in Somerset County. Increasing their speed, the engines plowed into the drift, hoping to power their way through. One by one, all four engines overturned. Two engineers and two firemen were

were trapped under the engines and killed. Escaping steam painfully scalded a third fireman. Other wrecks near Hackettstown, Flemington, and Jersey City claimed additional lives.

By Wednesday, March 14, the worst of the blizzard was over. Light, intermittent snow continued to fall, the winds remained brisk, but life began to return to normal. The railroads, hiring thousands of temporary workers, set about clearing their tracks. "At 11:10 A.M. [Wednesday] a loco-motive came from Jamesburg on the Pennsylvania Railroad," reported the *Monmouth Democrat.* "It . . . came tearing through [Freehold], shrieking hideously, puffing and straining and snorting like some terrible, infuriated wild beast. All of the machinery was covered with snow, and as it plunged through the snow banks it threw the snow in every direction completely

Figure 21. This Newark family happily poses in front of the greatest accu-mulation of snow they would ever see on their lifetimes. Felt in all of New Jersey's twenty-one counties, the blizzard claimed nearly one hundred lives. Courtesy of the Newark Public Library.

enclosing itself in a cloud. . . . More people than had been seen in three days gathered at the crossing in about half a minute to see the monster work through, and when it had passed followed it to the outskirts of town and watched it disappear into the distance. A little while after word was received that it had jumped the track at Howell and that both cylinder heads were cracked."

"Thousands of men worked all last night on the Pennsylvania Railroad, jacking engines back on the tracks, hauling snowbound trains out of the drifts and digging out the miles on miles of tracks," wrote the *Newark Evening News*. The "snow blockade" was finally broken, proclaimed the paper. "Up to noon to-day eight passenger trains had come out from New York on the Pennsylvania road to Market street, and all of them returned, jammed full of passengers. A Lehigh Valley train, which came out at nine o'clock started back at 9:15 with two engines ahead and one behind. When it left the depot men and boys were hanging on all of the platforms; passengers were sitting all around. The edge of the tender on the engine itself, the roofs of the cars, and even the cabs were jammed full. As the train rolled out of the depot the people on board yelled like demons and continued to do so until the train vanished from sight across the bridge at Commercial street."

In the cities, many trains and streetcars remained stalled, telegraph lines were down, and the few telephones then in service worked only intermittently. As Wednesday wore on, however, "the icy grip" of the storm loosened its hold. "The snow shovelers were early astir, and though they charged exorbitantly for their services they received a liberal patronage, and were soon clearing sidewalks or tunneling through snowdrifts," wrote the *Paterson Morning Call*. "By ten or eleven o'clock the main thoroughfares had been rendered passable, but the roadways still remained choked with the beautiful snow, and a horse and wagon was as rare a sight as would be a bible in a faro room. The streets presented a strange appearance, indeed. Piled high at the curb stones were the snow banks, increased in size by the snow thrown from the walks, while from curb to curb the roadways were filled knee-deep with . . . heaps of iridescent whiteness. The one staple and invaluable article of commerce was the snow shovel. Everywhere throughout the city there were men, boys and even women wielding it. The Erie and other railroad companies bought hundreds of snow shovels, and placed them in the hands of every individual who was willing to earn a dollar and a half a day by the sweat of his brow. Entrances to houses which had been completely blocked by snowdrifts were opened by the shovel brigades, the sidewalks were made navigably clean, and by noon it became possible for almost every one to take a walk around and see how his friends and neighbors had weathered the storm."

"The factory whistles and bells this morning indicated that industries had freed themselves from the blizzard's grasp, and the snow drifts in the streets are being beaten down by the sleighs and vehicles of market men and vendors of various articles of food and drink," said Elizabeth's *New Jersey Journal.* "The milkmen in many cases were still unable to get any milk this morning, owing to the non-arrival of the trains, and the news-men were without the New York newspapers till late." Bakers who the day before had struggled through the big snow drifts with huge baskets of bread and rolls, were now able to make "their usual early calls by means of sleighs, and hot buttered rolls gave cheer at the breakfast hour again to many dispirited citizens. The early pedestrians had little difficulty getting about the city. The idle business men and mechanics soon after the lull in the storm yesterday began to shovel off the snow and to cut footpaths through the drifts in front of their homes. In many places these drifts were higher than men's heads, and the pedestrians would be hidden at intervals as they walked through the cuts and . . . tunneled passage ways."

As the sun began to melt the snow, life slowly returned to normal. In Newark, "small boys on the hill in the neighborhood of Wallace Place stuck a hat on top of a heap of snow, and a few feet lower down imbedded a pair of boots, giving the appearance of a man buried in the drift with only his hat and feet in sight. The boys stood around the corner and enjoyed the looks of consternation on the faces of pedestrians and laughed at their efforts to extricate the suppositious man." Over on New Street, Policeman Van Riper arrested "a tall woman, respectably dressed, with a badly battered face." She was, said the *Evening News*, "overcome by drink and carried a fancy decanter partly filled with rum. This morning she was prostrated from the effects of her debauch. She gave her name as Lizzie Reynolds and said she had never drunk a drop of liquor before." She had been caught in the storm, she explained in Magistrate's Court, and only bought the liquor "to sustain life." An understanding judge dismissed all charges, gave Reynolds a nickel, and ordered her to take the streetcar home.

The Great September Gale—September 3, 1821

Hurricanes are the nastiest storms that most people in the mid-Atlantic states ever experience. Originating over warm tropical waters, these massive, rotating weather systems are defined by sustained winds of 74 miles per hour or more. The worst of them produce huge tidal surges, battering waves, drenching rainfall, and fearsome gales that leave a path of death and destruction in their wake. At the center of the rotation is the eye, an area of deceptive calm. Of the score or so hurricanes that tore across New Jersey in the nineteenth century, two were remarkable for their intensity and destructive power.

The storm that struck New Jersey in September 1821, although not as well documented as others, is the only hurricane ever to pass directly over the state's land mass while retaining its distinctive eye. Scientists classify it as a category 4 hurricane, probably the most severe to make landfall in New Jersey in the past 350 years.

On the morning of September 3, a storm that originated near the Cape Verde Islands struck Cape May, then roared north at more than 50 miles per hour a short distance inland from the coast. Following a path approximated by today's Garden State Parkway, the storm continued into Monmouth County and then took dead aim at the New York metropolitan area. Violent winds were felt as far west as Philadelphia and Newton,

while along the Jersey Shore the barrier islands endured a howling gale
that lasted two hours and may have reached 100 miles per hour. New York
Harbor experienced flooding unsurpassed in modern history.

Charles Ludlum, who lived in South Dennis, some twenty miles north
of the southernmost tip of Cape May, remembered the storm's ferocity
years later. "The morning of September 3d, 1821, commenced with a light
wind from the west . . . ," he told the *Cape May Spray.* "At about 9 o'clock
the wind hauled round to the southeast, steadily increasing. At 11 o'clock
it might be called a gale, at 12 it was blowing a hurricane with intermittent gusts that drove in doors and windows, blowing down outbuildings,
trees, fences and overflowing the marshes between the beach and mainland several feet." It was difficult to stand against the gale, recalled Ludlum,
adding that while there were no clouds to be seen, there was "a universal
haze like a thick fog." Salt spray driven inland "some miles" killed vegetation, vessels offshore foundered, woodland was ruined, and Cape May lost
from sixteen to twenty feet of beach to erosion. At the height of the storm,
reported another observer, the force of the wind actually drove the waters
of Delaware Bay across the peninsula, cutting off the lower portion of the
cape from the mainland.

Furman Ericson, said to be "a tall man," was on the meadows near
Delmont with his seven-year-old son when he noticed a storm surge
approaching. Hoisting his son on his back, Ericson ran for his life. "Before
they reached the upland, the water was nearly to his armpits," reports
David Ludlum in his *New Jersey Weather Book.* Elijah Miller, who lived on
the southern end of Dias Creek, hurried to the schoolhouse when he saw
the sky darken. Warning the teacher to close the school, Miller took his
children and "hustled them homeward by the main road as fast as their
feet could carry them. Looking back as they went up the hill they saw great
waves capped with foam where they had walked but a few minutes before."

As the hurricane moved up the Jersey coast, then sparsely popu-
lated, it flattened cedar trees on Long Beach Island, extensively damaged
a small port on Little Egg Harbor, blew over chimneys and tore apart

outbuildings in Monmouth County. One resident of Little Egg Harbor told the *Trenton Federalist* that the spray of salt water carried twelve to fourteen miles inland, killing plant life over a wide area. "Its effects upon vegetation was so powerful as to kill the leaves of trees, grass and herbs of various kinds," reported the newspaper. "He observed one orchard on his journey, the leaves of the trees of which, on the side towards the ocean, were turned brown and appeared as if scorched and dead, while, on the other side, not exposed to the storm, the leaves were as green and healthful as before the gale."

An estimated four inches of rain "descended in torrents, deluging our streets and cellars," said the *New Brunswick Fredonian*, and hurricaneforce winds wrecked small vessels in Perth Amboy harbor, including two sloops that sank. Passing to the east of Newark, the storm spared New Jersey's largest city from what could have been certain catastrophe. "The tremendous Gale which succeeded the rain on the 3d inst. and which has done immense damage for hundreds of miles along the coast, was experienced here," reported Newark's *Sentinel of Freedom*. "The rain descended in torrents, and the violence of the wind indicated as much of the hurricane as we ever recollect seeing. Thanks to a merciful Providence, the injury here is nothing in comparison to the lives lost and the destruction of property in other places. In this town and its vicinity, many of the fruit and ornamental trees have been mangled, and others uprooted. The apple orchards in particular have suffered, by having the fruit beaten off, and the trees prostrated. The fields of Indian corn have also been prostrated." In the countryside, forest trees that had stood for centuries were blown over and crops ready for harvesting destroyed.

Though on the edge of the hurricane, Newton took a severe beating. The *Sussex Register* recorded a "very severe gale of wind from the S.E., accompanied with heavy wind" which knocked over fences, uprooted and twisted the largest trees, leveled corn and buckwheat crops, and destroyed fruit orchards.

After swirling up the coast, the hurricane took dead aim at New York Harbor. The weather began changing at nine in the morning, recounted the local newspapers, when the sky darkened and a heavy rain accompanied by thunder and lightning began to fall. Gale-force winds—"the most tremendous we ever witnessed"—continued to blow until 7:30 P.M. when suddenly the winds veered to the northwest, the clouds were swept away, and the stars began to twinkle in the sky, leaving behind damage never seen before. When it was over, more than fifty vessels had been wrecked, wharves on both sides of the Hudson River smashed, church steeples toppled, and buildings near the water's edge reduced to kindling. A thirteen-foot storm surge struck what is now known as Battery Park, the highest ever recorded in the harbor.

"The gale at this place was most awful and tremendous," wrote a Jersey City correspondent for the *New-Jersey Journal*. "Our wharves, docks, piers, etc. all swept away. Ship *Vulcan*, that lay at one of the piers, went high and dry on one of the broken docks. Sloop *Stephen* is ashore, stern and bow knocked in. Schooner *Enterprise*, schooner *Eliza*, pettiauger *Rosemond*, are complete wrecks. Four or five small craft stove to pieces. Loss of the steam boat company very great. Their wood washed away and small rowboats stove. The steamboat lay in the slip, and by keeping steam on her and playing the engine off shore, was saved without damage."

In 1815, Isaac Edge had erected a seven-story gristmill on the banks of the Hudson River near present-day Exchange Place. Although the fortress-like brownstone tower suffered no damage, its fifty-foot-long arms were shredded. "The windmill received extensive injury, all four of the arms or sails are gone, the small fly wheels torn off and the cap on top of the mill splintered and torn in many places," continued the *Journal*. "The trees in Grand st. almost all lie prostrate. Some roofs and chimneys blown down, one or two houses overturned, and the docks washed away. A large topsail schooner ashore in the cove, high and dry." Similar damage was reported at Hoboken, where docks and bridges were washed away, roofs torn off houses, and so much debris flew through the air that it was dangerous to be outside. Most roads were rendered impassable by downed trees and broken branches. At Communipaw village, a ship was beached, houses flattened, and trees knocked over.

Although the number of killed and injured by the hurricane of 1821 is unknown, accounts of the storm's violence make it certain that the toll was considerable, mostly by drowning when vessels in the path of the storm were swamped. Nearly twenty sailors were lost off the coast of Rockaway Beach, and a small boat "in which were a number of colored people, returning from a camp meeting near Woodbury, was overset and five of the people drowned" in the Delaware River. The *New York Evening Post* reported that seven sailors from a U.S. Navy vessel docked in the Jersey City harbor were missing and presumed drowned when their launch overturned. After leaving New Jersey, the hurricane headed toward Connecticut, where winds between 75 and 100 miles per hour left a trail of devastation. The storm finally blew itself out in western Massachusetts.

Statewide Hurricane—September 10–13, 1889

By the time New Jersey's next big hurricane struck, the 1821 storm had long been forgotten. The nor'easter that battered the state on September 10–13, 1889, left its mark on a 123-mile-long coastline vastly different from the deserted beaches of an earlier day. The barrier islands were now crowded with summer resorts from Sandy Hook south to Cape May. Billed as the "City by the Sea," Atlantic City's permanent population of about thirteen thousand swelled four- and fivefold as trainloads of day-trippers arrived for a sunny outing at the shore. Long Branch, Asbury Park, and Cape May, far less flamboyant, attracted visitors for longer stays.

The Jersey Shore's popularity dates to the post–Civil War years, when increasing prosperity and better transportation made vacationing a genuine possibility for working people. New rail links to New York, Camden, and Philadelphia brought a surge of visitors, including seven U.S.

presidents. Mansions, cottages, hotels, bathhouses, bulkheads, piers, and amusement parks dotted the shoreline. Hurricanes that buffeted the shore in 1876 and 1878 and caused extensive beach erosion and widespread damage failed to discourage either the crowds or the investors who rebuilt after each storm.

The hurricane of 1889, the most impressive of the nineteenth century's many storms, extended from Cape Hatteras to Nova Scotia. Its winds, clocked at more than 56 miles per hour along the New Jersey coastline and as high as 37 miles per hour in New York City, were accompanied by prodigious rainfall, as much as five inches in the metropolitan area. High tides and howling winds pushed a historic volume of water against the Atlantic coast and kept it there for four days.

"The first indication of approaching storms came on Friday last, when, although the day was as fair and clear as one could wish, an unusually high sea was rolling," reported the Asbury Park *Shore Press*. "All day Saturday the force of the waves increased. On Sunday the wind began, and by nightfall a gale was blowing all along the coast. It was a stiff northeast wind that viciously churned the high rolling breakers and sent them foam flecked, carrying destruction in their front. Sunday night, Monday and Monday night the gale continued, the wind changing only in the increasing intensity of its force. On Tuesday morning the storm had attained probably its greatest strength. Rain began to fall in sheets and torrents. The wind had slightly changed its quarter and was rushing down from almost due north, its musketry of sand and finely driven rain making progress against its force almost impossible. Indeed, only the most venturesome braved the storm-king's fury, and went to the beach to note the havoc that was rapidly being accomplished along our famed [boardwalk]. . . . The billows, tossed up by the cyclonic force, twisted and tore the solidest planking like so much paper, twisted iron railings into a thousand shapes and made deep-set pilings quiver to their bottom.

"The sand was strewn with masses of seaweed, in which could be seen thousands of muscles torn from their bed in some far-out ocean depth," continued the paper. "The foaming, roaring water was almost as black as ink, forming a background against which the breakers showed with livid whiteness. The wind seized each whitecap as it broke, and dashed it into the finest spray, which carried in great white clouds down the coast. Overhead the unbroken masses of leaden clouds, with cumulated mountains of black storm clouds, went driving by, discharging unceasingly their enormous stores of waters. All of Tuesday and Wednesday the storm's fury continued at its highest notch, there being no appreciable diminution until late Wednesday night."

Further north, the sustained gale-force winds, which reminded many of the blizzard that had paralyzed the region only eighteen months before, flooded the Meadowlands with more than four feet of water. Factory buildings, railroad bridges, and telegraph poles were blown over in Elizabeth. The flood tide reached the woods bordering Roselle, houses in Carteret were submerged to the second floor, and the lumber docks at the mouth of the Elizabeth River were inundated. Tens of thousands of dollars' worth of lumber stacked on the docks broke loose to float across the nearby meadows. At Elizabethport, shipping at the coal wharves was suspended when the tide swept over the piers, washing tons of valuable coal into the churning sea. Two fully loaded coal barges sank.

The storm's effect on the exposed coastline was devastating. Although no lives were lost in New Jersey, damage was in the millions. The worst destruction was north of Long Branch at Monmouth Beach and Sea Bright and along the length of the Sandy Hook peninsula and from Point Pleasant south to Cape May. From Long Branch south to Manasquan, the impact was confined to beachfront structures. At Sandy Hook and Highland Beach, nearly every building was damaged. A mile north of the beach the surging sea cut a new inlet one hundred feet wide through the hook, turning it into an island. "A stout bay horse and a strong buckboard, with a careful driver" took a New York Tribune reporter from Sea Bright to the new inlet cut through the peninsula above Highland Beach. "The old turnpike was covered with wreckage of all kinds, including spars, railroad

Figure 22. Engraving titled "A Scene of Destruction at Low Moor, near Long Branch, during the Storm." From *Harper's Weekly*, September 21, 1889.

sleepers and steel rails, boxes and barrels and all kinds of timbers," wrote the reporter. "The track of the Sandy Hook branch of the Central Railroad of New Jersey was covered with sand to a depth of four to seven feet from the Hotel Shrewsbury nearly to the Highland Beach station, two miles distant. The bulkheads erected a few years ago on the east side of the railroad tracks showed marked effects of the fury of the storm. They were completely torn to pieces, and the heavy oak planks and stout chestnut piling were scattered all over the road. The railroad station at Navesink Beach was almost completely wrecked.... The old turnpike has been obliterated. Many of the telegraph poles had fallen down and the iron wires were hanging loose and swinging in the wind. A short distance south of the Highland Beach railroad station the track was twisted into all sorts of shapes. A number of bathing houses stood upon their roofs in the sand."

Sea Bright was heavily damaged, the Shrewsbury River rose to unprecedented heights, flooding buildings along its bank, and at Red Bank docks were shattered and pleasure boats driven ashore. The boiling surf undermined large sections of the famous bluff at Long Branch, toppling it into the ocean. Asbury Park, Ocean Grove, Avon-by-the-Sea, and Belmar saw all their piers, beach houses, and bathing pavilions battered into floating wreckage. Railroad tracks were washed out, telegraph lines knocked down, and roads covered with sand. Communication was cut off for days. The barrier islands south of Point Pleasant were inundated as the wind-driven waves broke over them, joining the waters of the bay. Sea Isle City was completely submerged, its boardwalk torn away, hotels and cottages wrecked, and Townsend's Inlet bridge undermined. Ocean City, Avalon, Wildwood, and Cape May were heavily damaged.

Surrounded by the sea, Atlantic City suffered the most. Towering waves tore at the beach, breaking as far inland as Pacific Avenue. At high tide the ocean waters extended to Atlantic Avenue, flooding hotels and boarding houses filled with terrified guests. Houses along Baltic and Mediterranean Avenues were under water to the second floor and a fire, perhaps incendiary, destroyed a block of hotels and houses. City water and sewerage plants were shut down. Food grew scarce. When the meadows behind the city flooded, all train traffic was halted, cutting the city off from the mainland. "Atlantic City is in a sadly wrecked condition," reported the *Philadelphia Inquirer*. "While no lives have been lost, the damage by storm is beyond all comprehension. . . . The waves have not only torn away the boardwalk, but they have swept into ruin nearly everything along the ocean front. A portion of the great iron pier has been demolished. . . . Pavilions, bath houses, restaurants, booths have been torn asunder. The beach is a mass of ruins. Great holes have been eaten out of the sand, while high tides have covered many portions of the city."

"The whole sea front of Atlantic City is torn out," Captain Edward A. Langdon told the Philadelphia paper. "The merry-go-rounds, the restaurants, stores, booths and other property along the boardwalk are entirely swept away. I had a restaurant there on the boardwalk, and had begun packing up my goods when the storm came. The restaurant building is a complete wreck, and I am out to the tune of $580." Langdon claimed it was "the worst storm I ever saw in my life, and I have been down to Atlantic City since before 1876. . . . The waves came rushing up to the boardwalk with a fury that was simply awful, and many a man is as ruined as I am. The piers along the shore are wrecked and all the streets are covered . . . to a depth of three feet at the lowest and many feet at the highest point of flood. The excursion house is surrounded by water and the downpour and waves have invaded every house on the beach and most of the houses inland. The big hotels on the ocean front are being torn away piecemeal, and unless this storm ceases there won't be left a whole stick in Atlantic City."

On Monday night, thousands of stranded visitors lined Pacific Avenue watching "with awe the mountainous waves beat upon the shore." As the storm grew in intensity, the hotels along Atlantic Avenue were evacuated as a precaution. At midnight the cry of "fire" was heard. Lee's Ocean Terrace, a complex of hotels below Texas Avenue, had fallen into the water earlier that evening. Now it was burning. As "frightened and nervous hotel guests were endeavoring to get a few hours' rest, a sheet of flame was seen to shoot up from the ruined buildings," the *New York Times* reported. "It was a period of terror for these people, and when they anxiously peered through their windows and saw the sky illumined with red glare of fire, they sprang from their beds and rushed pell mell to the lower floors, most of them in their night attire. They imagined the flames were close upon them, and the strongest assurances had no quieting effect. A guest at the Mansion House, where there were over 250 people, the greater number being women and children, describes the midnight scene: 'The women came rushing down stairs with blanched faces, wringing their hands and crying as if the day of Judgment had come. Outside banging shutters, creaking signs, the howling hurricane, the hiss and swish of the swaying trees, the rushing banging fire engines, and the general commotion attending a fire at night struck terror into the hearts of these women and they huddled together in the parlors and prayed and sobbed and listened to the consoling words of the

Figure 23. Guests watch the 1889 hurricane from the porch of Atlantic City's
Brighton Hotel. From *Harper's Weekly*, September 21, 1889.

men, who knew full well that the danger was still far off. The fright of these
people was not ended until the fire on the Ocean Terrace had consumed
the wrecked buildings."

"When dreary nightfall enveloped the city almost every foot of it was
submerged, the flood varying in depth from one to five feet," wrote a *New*

York Tribune reporter at the scene. "This morning [the 12th] even the oldest residents, who had weathered many a severe storm on this exposed
island, hurried along the streets with blanched faces and anxious looks,
eagerly scanning the horizon for a hopeful indication that the storm
would soon be over. Many of them had large property interests at stake,
and their early morning mission was to see to what extent the waves and
wind had damaged their holdings. Then the hotel guests put in an appearance, the women wrapped in shawls and gossamers and the men clad in
storm coats, gum boots and close-fitting caps. . . . The weird storm had
lost its fascination. They were no longer bent on sightseeing. Their one
great object was to get away from the desolate surroundings, back to their
comfortable city homes, safe from the warring elements. So they hurried
to the railroad stations as if their lives depended on the alacrity of their
movements. They rushed pell-mell into the cars."

Despite the fact that the tracks were under a foot or more of water, four
trains packed with frightened passengers made an attempt to reach the
mainland. "Each had a locomotive in the front and one in the rear when
they headed for the flooded meadowland, and they crept along over the
hidden tracks as if fearful of a fatal plunge," wrote the reporter. "They all
went out between the hours of 6 and 9 in the morning, just as the high tide
was nearing its limit. The hurricane, too, was gaining in strength, and its
fierce, sweeping gusts threw the water against the car windows and made
the heavy coaches rock to and fro as if in momentary danger of overturning. It was then that a feeling of terror filled the indiscreet passengers, who
only a short time before were gleeful in their anticipations of a speedy
escape from a submerged town."

None of the trains reached the mainland. "Their engines were plough-
ing through two to four feet of water, which threatened every moment
to extinguish the fires, and as there was a veritable sea ahead, there was
no alternative but to return. So the engines were reversed and the trip
back begun, now doubly hazardous because of the fact that the waters had
risen several inches. Hardly a furlong had been covered, however, before

the fires were extinguished by the rushing torrents of water, which dashed against the cars with terrific force, breaking the windows and completely enveloping the trains in spray."

When the trains stalled there was, said the *Tribune*'s reporter, "a scene of consternation . . . that beggars description. Women screamed and fainted, children cried, and stouthearted men gave way to the general despair. All efforts to relieve the general despondency seemed unavailing, and it was only when the conductors went from car to car and shouted themselves hoarse to the effect that relief engines had been telegraphed for that the frightened passengers resumed a more hopeful air and patiently awaited the approach of their rescuers. When they did come it took a mighty effort to pull the beleaguered trains over the sunken and twisted tracks, and it was 3 o'clock in the afternoon before the last trainload of passengers was pulled slowly into the Camden and Atlantic station. Then the announcement was made that no trains would leave tonight and probably none tomorrow."

The hurricane stalled offshore, then turned southwest, punishing the coast with high winds for nearly four days. According to a shore historian, the tide was "the highest and most destructive in the history of Atlantic City." The storm surge on the Jersey coast was the largest in more than forty years. "For three days terror reigned from Sea Bright to Long Branch, and no one felt secure within 500 feet of the mad rage of the ocean," wrote the *Jersey Journal*. "From Sandy Hook to Cape May, the ruin wrought on this coast will make a permanent change in the shoreline. . . . All the pretty villages so popular for seaside summering were woefully devastated by the great waves." At sea, thirty-one vessels were wrecked with an estimated loss of forty lives.

New Brunswick Tornado—June 19, 1835

"A full view of the funnel of a mature tornado is one of nature's most awesome spectacles," writes David M. Ludlum in *The New Jersey Weather*

Book. "No refuge above ground assures full protection from its wrath. Property destruction can be almost complete in a limited area when a full-developed funnel sweeps the surface of the earth; human life is placed in great jeopardy from devastating wind blasts, flying objects that become deadly missiles, and collapsing buildings." The black cloud tinged with a sickly yellow hue, the thunder and lightning, the hail stones and spiraling wind-borne debris that are the hallmark of the killer tornadoes periodically wreaking havoc in the Mississippi River Valley are a rare sight in New Jersey. Of the twelve full-fledged tornadoes documented by newspapers and state meteorologists during the nineteenth century, only four would enter the record books because of their destructive power: the 1835 tornado that swept through the heart of New Brunswick killing five people and leveling hundreds of buildings; a short-lived but powerful storm that destroyed a solid brick factory building near Camden twenty-five years later, killing three; a massive tornado that ripped through Philadelphia, Camden, and Bucks County in 1885, causing $500,000 worth of damage; and a smaller but equally violent storm that wrecked the small Bergen County village of Cherry Hill in 1895.

The New Brunswick tornado of June 19, 1835, began life as a hailstorm at Ringoes, then traveled on an erratic northeasterly course through Middlebush, New Brunswick, Piscataway, and Perth Amboy, finally petering out over Staten Island, where another hailstorm flattened newly planted crops. People in New Brunswick first noticed the storm as it approached a hill at the western edge of town where, according to the *New Brunswick Times*, "it remained apparently fixed for a minute or two, presenting the appearance of a pillar of fire—its base resting on the earth, and its top reaching a mass of black clouds. It then took an eastern course, threatening Albany and Church streets, but suddenly changed its direction, swept across the town lot towards [several dwellings], tearing the roofs off some, making literal wrecks of the barns and outhouses, and either uprooting or twisting off the largest trees—in some instances carried the latter 20 or 30 paces." The tornado tore through Paterson,

Liberty, Bayard, and Schureman Streets, reported the *Times*, lifting roofs off houses and flattening stores. Nicholas Booraem, a lawyer, and his eldest son, Henry, were buried under the wreckage. "Both were extricated a short time after—the son in a dying state, in which he lingered until 9 o'clock, when death relieved him from his suffering. . . . A young lad of about 8 years of age, son of Capt. Baird, was killed near this spot, a rafter from the blacksmith's shop having struck him immediately above the eyes, and almost severed his head.

"The tornado now swept with increased force across George street, down Liberty, Schureman, and New streets, crossing Nelson to Burnet street, a quarter of a mile distance down to the river, unroofing or tearing off the tops of the houses, and sweeping the lower floors and windows from their fastenings," continued the newspaper report. "Schureman and Liberty streets, from top to bottom, may be said to be a complete mass of ruins, as is likewise part of Burnet street. The Methodist church, a brick edifice, is damaged beyond repair, having been unroofed, and the eastern and southern walls blown down; and the rear wall of the Catholic church, also of brick, is drove into the body of the building."

After leaving New Brunswick, the tornado tracked the Raritan River a short distance, then crossed and passed over several farms, tearing up trees by their roots and demolishing homes and barns. It then struck Piscataway, a village of about a dozen houses, wrecking every building save two, including the Episcopal church. Thomas W. Harper, a New York silversmith who happened to be in Piscataway inspecting property he had just purchased, was killed when a beam struck him on the head.

Contemporary newspaper accounts of the tornado record its bizarre behavior. "Among the extraordinary occurrences which took place on this melancholy occasion, the fate of the son of Wm. G. Dunham (a small lad) was the most singular," wrote a *New York Gazette* reporter. "He was taken off the piazza of the house, corner of New and George streets, carried in the air a distance of 300 yards, and landed on the wharf in Burnet street, having only sustained a slight injury in one of his arms. On being questioned as to his feelings, he stated that he recollected passing through the top of a willow tree, and that the sensation produced by being carried up in the whirlwind was like that of being pulled in contrary directions. A bedstead was taken from the third story of a house in Schureman street, carried a distance of 200 yards, and landed in Burnet street, without having sustained the slightest injury. A carpet bag and some bedding were carried from the garret of Dr. Janeway's house to the river, a distance of nearly half a mile."

"The first intimation I had of the tornado's approach was the wind blowing in from both sides of the house in which I was sitting," said an eyewitness. "Immediately the cry of fire was raised—I ran to the corner of the street and perceived in a westerly direction, at about half a mile's distance, a black column moving onward, not very rapidly, which had something the appearance of a smothered fire, and was mistaken for it. I saw what it was and ran into the house and closed all the windows before it reached us. The whole atmosphere was filled with fragments of timber, &c—in a moment the house opposite was unroofed, as if it had been covered with paper. The house in which I was, being at the edge of the current, escaped uninjured, save that a rafter from the roof of a house about half a mile distant, thirty feet long, struck the edge of the window, tearing away the brick work and demolishing the sash, and passed into the wall of the room."

According to estimates at the time, the New Brunswick tornado destroyed more than 150 buildings. Overall losses exceeded $100,000.

Camden Tornado—July 26, 1860

A brief but extremely violent tornado that lifted a substantial brick factory building from its foundation about a mile east of central Camden on July 26, 1860, struck without warning. Messrs. Potts and Klett had just completed their new chemical works near the Cooper River, on the Haddonfield road, today's Haddon Avenue, near the railroad tracks. Their two-story building, "pronounced by experienced architects to be perfectly safe," measured 200 by 36 feet. Built of brick with walls twenty-two inches thick, reinforced by pilasters inside and out and capped by a heavy slate roof, it was, said the *Philadelphia Press*, "one of the most durable, as well as one of the most complete establishments in the country." At about a quarter after three in the afternoon Potts, Klett, and their bookkeeper were working in an office in the northern part of the building. Eight laborers were clearing construction debris from other parts of the building, getting it ready for the new machinery.

A heavy clap of thunder accompanied by lightning and hail announced the tornado's arrival. "The shock was so severe that it appeared to shake the building to its centre, and simultaneously with the shock the entire building, with the exception of the northern end, was moved from its foundation, and turned almost completely around from the southeast to the northwest," wrote the newspaper. "The laborers, through fear of being buried in the ruins, jumped out of the windows, and as they did so portions of the heavy walls fell upon them." Three workers were killed, four injured. "Messrs. Potts and Klett retained their seats in their office, and although conscious of the danger surrounding them, deemed it more prudent to do so than to run the risk of being crushed by the falling walls. The tornado lasted but a few minutes, and uprooted several large trees and a number of small buildings in the neighborhood. The noise produced was heard a great distance from the scene of the disaster."

A group of men driving along the Haddonfield Road about a mile from the chemical works told the reporter that "when they first heard the clap of thunder they noticed something like a pillar of fire revolving in the sky, and almost simultaneously were started by the falling of the walls of the building." A tornado that could wreck a large, heavily reinforced brick building would be ranked an EF5 on today's Enhanced Fujita scale, with winds of more than 200 miles per hour. In spite of its losses, estimated at $4,000, Potts and Klett Manufacturing Chemists was soon back in business, producing dyes and other chemicals in a large complex between Pine and Line Streets until the mid-1880s.

Camden Tornado—August 3, 1885

A quarter of a century later, the Camden-Philadelphia area was again struck by a destructive tornado. On the afternoon of August 3, 1885, a large funnel was observed crossing the Delaware River from Philadelphia near the present site of the Walt Whitman Bridge. After battering two steamboats in the river, the tornado destroyed buildings along the Camden riverfront, then crossed the river again to strike the Port Richmond area of North Philadelphia. Heading north through Bucks County, where it tore through a cemetery in Churchville, "demolishing all the tombstones, monuments and railings," the storm then went on to drop historic amounts of rainfall on Port Jervis, New York, and Easton, Pennsylvania. In the Camden-Philadelphia area, more than five hundred buildings were damaged, six people killed, and more than one hundred injured. Property losses in Camden alone exceeded $500,000.

"The cyclone was first observed advancing at a marvelously rapid rate across the Delaware River from Greenwich Point," reported the *Philadelphia Inquirer*. "It looked first like a dark rain cloud, from which a heavy rain was pouring upon the earth so dense that everything around it looked black. Dark clouds were approaching at the same time from the southeast, and at a point directly over the roofs of the property of the Pennsylvania Salt Company at Greenwich Point, the rain column and the black clouds from the southwest seemed to meet. Immediately the tall column began to whirl with a frightful velocity, accompanied by the roar of a hurricane that could be heard in the distance. Buildings at the salt works were demolished in the space of a minute, and fragments of them and even whole roofs were carried high in the air and scattered around like shavings." From the salt works the storm moved in a northeasterly direction toward Kaighn's Point, Camden, attacking the steamboat, *Major Reybold*, "spreading havoc and devastation over the decks of the steamer in a way that could not have been more complete if it had been raked with the fire of a cannon. Old river men who witnessed the sight say they never saw anything to equal it in their lives. . . . The sweeping demon in the air whirled to the banks of the Jersey shore, and everywhere havoc, ruin, and devastation were strewn in its path."

The tornado kept to the Jersey side of the river until it reached a point opposite Port Richmond, continued the newspaper account. "Here it swept across the stream again driving vessels from their moorings, unroofing houses, demolishing buildings, resulting in the loss of one life and the injury of sixteen persons. All the work of ruin along the length and breadth of the cyclone's track was all done probably in the space of a quarter of an hour. There was no rain at the time, and only a light breeze blowing."

The tornado's path was an estimated five hundred feet wide, according to news accounts. "Its appearance was that of a dense black cloud revolving at terrific rate. In the heart of it the gloom was like the darkness of midnight, and eyewitnesses describe the air as so black that they could not see their hands before their faces. The bottom of it moved over the river like a rolling ball of smoke. The phenomenal force of the wind can only be imagined from the visible evidence of its destruction, and its power seemed to be almost supernatural. . . . After the cyclone passed, a heavy rain storm set in, which lasted during the early part of the evening, with frequent sharp flashes of lightning."

A reporter from the *Inquirer* who climbed to one of the upper floors of Philadelphia's Pennsylvania Railroad Building called the tornado "a great but terrible sight." It approached, he wrote, "in the shape of a huge black cloud, driving before it a lighter funnel-shaped mass that seemed like spray or a densely compacted snow squall. Its course was not directly up the river, but across it in a diagonal line, which included two or three miles of the river in its course. The cloud rushed along with terrible velocity, but never at the same height. It alternately sank so low as to touch the earth and then rose again to a considerable height, the alternate dipping and rising occurring within the course of perhaps three or four hundred yards. Whenever the cloud dropped there was sure to be an upheaval, and with it a roof would go flying off.

"A roof when struck would be lifted straight up for quite a distance, resembling a piece of black felt, and then, after being twisted around and around and hurled along with frightful rapidity, would break into a thousand pieces," the reporter continued. "In their fall the pieces resembled the breaking up of a barrel, the staves tumbling in every imaginable shape. . . . This lifting of roofs seemed to continue all along the Jersey shore from a point somewhere near Kaighn's Point avenue to Cooper's Point, after which it moved to the westward crossing again into Port Richmond." Railroad clerks at work in the building were panic-stricken. "They rushed to the windows and with breathless awe gazed intently on the mass of broken materials whirling in the cyclone's bosom. At other time fences, roofs, and trees went sailing aloft and circling around like so many feathers. Several tin roofs stripped bodily from the houses in the southern part of Camden, were noticed sailing about with the rest. The awful sight lasted less than ten minutes, but will never be forgotten by those who witnessed it."

A Philadelphia police officer said that "it looked to him like two clouds advancing rapidly to meet each other." Looking over to the New Jersey shore, he saw pieces of timber and trees tumbling through the air. Another witness said that when the gale was at its height, "the clouds looked like an immense volume of smoke. In the center was visible a flag, apparently attached to a staff which had been torn off a building. A tin roof was seen flying through the air with such velocity that it at first resembled the flight of a flock of pigeons."

The western portion of Camden, from the Delaware River to Third Street, and from as far south as Kaighn Avenue to half a mile above the Camden and Atlantic Railroad depot, at Cooper's Point, was wrecked in less than five minutes. "About half past three o'clock a roaring sound as of the ocean in a storm, or a long train of cars traveling over a bridge at some distance away, was heard by the citizens rumbling down the Delaware," according to another account in the *Inquirer*. "It approached closer and closer every second, the rumbling being mixed with the crackling and twisting sound of woodwork wrenched from the houses as it got nearer. Then the air, which had been filled with moisture and rain all the afternoon, suddenly grew darker and darker and pieces of wood at first fell before the astonished vision of those whose position commanded a view.

"Up Second street, and from there to the Delaware, the sound came increasing in intensity and power. Terror-stricken women and children and even strong men ran in every direction from the approaching horror that seemed to take on two aspects as it appeared on the shore and on the water. Along the latter it assumed the shape of a waterspout in the form of a huge screw that twisted and turned as it passed northward. Along the shore, up Front and Second, it was a veritable cyclone of frightful force."

Newspaper stories tell of houses unroofed, large trees wrenched up by their roots and hundreds of telephone and telegraph poles down, their wires twisted in "hopeless confusion." Substantial, three-story brick factory buildings were flattened, the West Jersey Railroad's roundhouse was leveled, freight trains overturned, a large three-masted schooner in dry dock twisted in half, heavy industrial machinery tossed into the air, and windows and walls blown out. The tornado plowed through the city in a zigzag pattern, skipping some blocks and thoroughly demolishing others.

"The suffering of thousands of families last night who occupied houses in the track of the tornado was sorrowful to witness," reported the *Philadelphia Inquirer*. "Rain poured in torrents in the roofless houses, deluging the terror-stricken inhabitants, who were almost powerless to protect themselves. The furniture of those who were unable to procure wagons to carry them to places of shelter, was piled up in heaps in the rooms and carpets thrown over them to keep them as dry as possible. When wagons could be procured the household goods were removed to empty houses in other parts of the city. The citizens whose houses were spared opened them to the unfortunates, providing them with shelter and food." Homeowners unable to store their household goods anywhere else were allowed to use the Sixth Regiment Armory.

The tornado caught the steamboat *Major Reybold* in mid-river, nearly sinking it. The steamer, which made daily trips from Philadelphia to Salem and back, had fifty passengers onboard, far fewer than normal, owing to the day's stormy weather. With Captain Eugene Reybold of Philadelphia and pilot Emory Townsend of Salem in the pilothouse, the *Major Reybold* left the dock at 3:00 P.M. in a heavy downpour. Less than thirty minutes later, the *Inquirer* reported, "the captain caught sight of the long cloud-like column of air sweeping towards the river from the southeast. At first it looked like a thick mass of pouring rain, black as midnight and furious and angry looking. It swept across the river with extraordinary speed until it reached Greenwich Point, and then a terrible scene of destruction could be seen by those aboard the steamer. The wicked black mass of clouds began to whirl and twist like a corkscrew. In the midst of it could be seen the flying and splintering timber of the roofs of houses. . . . Heavy beams, fragments of floors and walls went up, and were torn to shreds high in the air."

Captain Reybold, who knew in an instant he was heading into a tornado, immediately steered in the direction of the Jersey shoreline to avoid the danger. But the storm zigzagged toward his vessel as if following it. "We're going to get it," shouted the captain, standing at the port side of the wheel, and then, leaning all his weight on the wheel, he shouted again to the pilot, Townsend, "Haul for the Jersey shore!"

"Even then we could hear the dull ominous roar above the steady stroke of the engine and the splash of the paddle wheels," recalled Reybold later. "It was sweeping down on us with the speed of lightning, and the whole thing didn't last more than two minutes. If it had we would have all gone down to the bottom with a split hull. . . . I shoved the windows down in the pilot house, and told Townsend to put them down on his side, or the roof would be carried off like a hen coop.

"Then the roaring came on us like a frightful blast from a furnace," explained the captain. "There was no rain, and the air, which was perfectly clear but a few moments before, grew black as midnight. I could only catch a dim glance of Townsend's face. It was as white as death, and his eyes were staring at me in fright. I thought he was going to drop, and in the terrible noise and fury of the tornado I shouted, 'My God, don't let go of that wheel!' That was the last thing I said. We were carried up and the next thing I knew I was going down, down in the water. I never saw Townsend after I shouted to him at the wheel."

Captain Reybold narrowly escaped drowning. "He struggled to the surface of the water, under the weight of a gum coat and thick boots," reported the newspaper. "When his head came out of the water he was struck by the paddlewheel of the steamer and almost knocked insensible beneath the surface again. He came up next under a lot of floating timber and wrecked cabins. He succeeded in working his coat off and kicked one of his boots off. Exhausted from his exertions and bleeding from cuts on his face and hands, he was finally rescued by the deck hands of the steamboat *Jersey Blue.*"

Pandemonium reigned on the *Reybold* when the tornado struck. While the captain, the pilot, and some of the deck hands had a premonition of what was about to happen, most of the passengers and crew on the after part of the boat had no warning until the terrible force of the tornado struck them. "Nearly all of the passengers were in the cabin on the lower deck. They knew nothing until the air around them grew black and the terrible roaring of the tornado struck terror in every soul on board.

"Women and children screamed and clutched wildly at anything they could get hold of for support. Above the roar the cracking of timber, the tearing of ironwork and the crash and confusion of freight tumbling about on deck could be heard like the rumbling of doom. It was an awful moment. In the dark no one could be recognized, and, to make the scene, such as it was, more terrifying, the groans and cries of wounded men blended in the tumult.

"Cabin doors were torn from their hinges, glass frames and partitions were smashed, and the woodwork above the deck was torn out of the joints and whirled into the air. The steamer's heavy iron smokestack was twisted from its fastenings like a tin pipe and hurled into the river almost at the same moment the pilot house went over.

"When the fury, which lasted but a few seconds, but which to those terrified people on the boat seemed ages, had passed, a scene of unutterable confusion was revealed," continued the news account. "Men and women stood around with their senses partially dazed, and staring wildly at the wreck and demolition around them. The water was pouring over the decks, and cabin sides were stove, the upper deck and roof were carried away, and the rain poured down in torrents on the passengers, who had not a board left to shelter them. For a time the screaming and running about and fainting women prevented anyone getting an intelligent idea of what had happened. Everything above the hull deck was in ruins. . . .

"Passengers ran about with their faces bleeding. The steamer itself was a wreck. Nothing remained above decks but the engine shaft, the walking beam, the paddle boxes and the woodwork around the boiler. The upper decks and cabin were gone. Below only the wooden sides of the cabin were standing. The furniture, seat cushions and interior framework were carried away."

Two tugboats towed the disabled steamboat to Philadelphia's Arch Street wharf. Damage to the *Major Reybold* was estimated at $5,000. Townsend, the pilot, had drowned. Five passengers and crew were seriously injured.

Cherry Hill Tornado—July 13, 1895

The lethal tornadoes that hopscotched across New Jersey on July 13, 1895, almost wiped the tiny Bergen County village of Cherry Hill off the map. What the American Meteorological Society's journal clinically described as "a series of atmospheric disturbances, partaking of the nature of severe

wind and hail storms in some places, and in others of tornadic movements" damaged crops and fruit trees from Cape May to the Atlantic High-
lands. At Red Bank, hailstones as large as walnuts fell; from Annandale to
North Branch the hail damaged the corn crop and pressed grain down to
the ground. In Plainfield, Susan R. Van Winkle and her fiancé, Leonard
Smith, were sitting in her parlor addressing invitations to their wedding
when the storm struck. According to press reports, "Miss Van Winkle, at
the approach of the storm, was seized with hysterics . . . , gradually grew
worse" and died an hour later. In Ridgewood, centuries-old trees toppled
over and apple orchards were stripped of their fruit. "The Hohokus Valley
Tennis Club was all ready for its regular Saturday afternoon tea," reported
a Newark newspaper. "The tent was up, the ladies in their places and the
players about to begin. In ten minutes every piece of china had been
destroyed, the tent torn into ribbons and the courts strewn with branches
and twigs."

Cherry Hill (now part of River Edge) was a tiny village that hugged
the western shore of the Hackensack River six miles north of the county
seat. It was, said the *New York Times*, "as pretty a hamlet as there is in the
Hackensack Valley. There were about thirty houses, dotting the side of two
parallel streets, and as many crossroads. They were small suburban resi-
dences, some of them occupied by men whose business takes them into
the city every day, with well-kept lawns and large shade trees, and gardens and barns." Near the river stood a small train depot. Fruit orchards,
cornfields and truck gardens stretched off into the distance. Shortly before
4 P.M. a massive black cloud that suddenly gathered over Cherry Hill let
loose a storm of hail and rain followed by a tornado funnel. In a matter of
minutes three people were killed, nearly a hundred injured and the village
wrecked. Six buildings were reduced to splinters.

The town's deputy postmaster was standing in the doorway of the
post office when he first noticed a black cloud in the distance. The winds
were at first warm, he told the press afterward, then turned cold, followed
almost immediately by a cold rain intermingled with immense hailstones.

As the black cloud parted, a cloud of yellow burst into view. A terrific gust of wind, he said, threw him backward into the building.

Blacksmith John H. Jones also saw a thick black cloud approaching from the northwest. In the Reformed Church at the time, he was astonished at the dense blackness that descended on the village. Running outside, he came face to face with an oddly shaped cloud advancing toward him that seemed to be full of yellow light. "I ran across the street to Friedman's Hotel," Jones told a *New York Herald* reporter afterward, "and cried, 'Look out, there's a heavy gale coming.' I was so excited that I threw my tools on the floor, and went out to the door again to watch the storm. Just then something struck me on the head, and I was lifted up bodily and thrown into the ditch on the opposite side of the road. I did not lose consciousness, but crouched down in the ditch clinging to the grass. The big cloud that seemed full of yellow light spun round and round. Everything seemed to go round—dirt, bricks, wood, everything. I could see all that happened. I saw Friedman come flying out of the window of his hotel." Jones waited for a lull, then rushed toward the railroad tracks, hugging the ground there until the storm passed. "As I lay flat on my stomach I glanced around, and saw that my own house had been blown from its foundations and tilted back like a rocking chair. . . .

"In the meantime, Sexton George Himmel was having a terrifying experience in the Dutch Reformed Church," reported the *Herald*. "Sexton Himmel, nearly frightened to death, was in the church during all this hubbub. He was crouched behind the rail of the choir loft, expecting each moment to be his last. In the height of the blow a rafter 18 feet long, presumably blown from Friedman's hotel, crashed, end-on, into the wooden wall of the church not five feet from where he was hiding." All but two feet of the beam penetrated the church.

Opposite the New Jersey and New York Railway station stood Conrad Friedman's hotel, a popular tourist destination. "In the hotel at the time, besides the proprietor, were his wife and three children," reported the *New York Times*. "Just as the storm broke he hustled them into the street. He ran through the barroom, after taking the money from the cash drawer, intending to join his family. He had just reached the door in front when a whirlwind struck the building. The rear door was open, and the wind, rushing through, caught him as he was on the doorsill. Eyewitnesses say he was lifted from his feet and carried ten feet forward and then dropped to the ground. He lay there half a second, and then the building fell, burying him." Friedman was killed.

Nearby lived the Ahrens family, their eight-month-old infant asleep in his crib. "The house was unroofed and partly wrecked, and a flying stick struck the child on the side of the head," reported the paper. "One of its ears was severed from the head as completely as though by a surgeon's knife, and with as little tearing of the flesh. The child's skull was fractured." The father, a New York businessman, was on the way home when his train was delayed by the storm. It arrived at the wrecked Cherry Hill station just as the sun was breaking through the clouds. "The first sight that met his eyes was his ruined home. In the midst of the wreck he found his wife, who, by one of the freaks of the storm, escaped injury, sitting with the body of the child in her lap, talking to it."

"The first intimation we had of the storm was a gathering blackness in the sky," another resident told a reporter for the *Newark Daily Advertiser*. "Then came the sound like the roaring of thunder." At first he thought it was thunder, but "when I saw how steady it was, and that it kept getting louder and louder, I knew that it was something else. Did you ever see smoke and steam rising up together? Well, that's something like what I saw on the forward edge of the cloud, only the bulk of the cloud was far darker than steam. The little puffs that fringed the mass were like dirty smoke or dust. . . . Never before in the sky have I seen a color like that.

"My wits seemed to have left me until I heard somebody shout 'cyclone!'" the man continued. "Then I knew what was up and dug for shelter. You have heard about the silence that comes before an approaching storm. Well, I tell you, there was none of that. Above the roar I heard men shouting to each other to save themselves. I think I shall never forget one woman's shriek. 'O, God!' she cried. 'Save our house! Just save our house!' But her house went down. Another thing that is stamped on my brain just like a flash-light picture was a man's face. Who it was, I don't know. He went past me as fast as his legs could carry him, just like a wild man. He clutched in his hand a pail which I suppose he had used to water his horses. His features were so white and twisted up with terror that I don't think his own mother would have known him. He was shouting something, but it was lost in the roar of the storm.

"[The tornado] seemed to jump right at us," the man told the reporter. "It struck the town almost like a solid body. Hailstones came like grape shot and there was an awful pouring down of rain. I put my arm over my eyes and from that time till the greatest force of the storm was over I didn't know what happened to anybody or anything but myself, except from the sounds I heard. I was tossed and rolled around just as if a big mad bull was at me. The sound was just as though some big frame building was crashing down on the street by stories. A roar and a hum . . . filled up the short gaps between the crashes. When the crashing stopped I got up and staggered around to see if my family and friends were killed. I thought I must be about the only one left. The shouts and the shrieks I heard before the storm began again. Men were shouting for their wives and children and women shouted in terror. By and by, the shouts died away, all except those of the people who were hurt."

The tornado left behind a three-hundred-foot-wide path of destruction unlike anything ever seen in that part of New Jersey. "Along the swath cut by the storm the general appearance was that of a lumber and kindling yard, in wild disorder," said Newark's *Advertiser*. "A few houses in the wrecked district stood intact. Others looked as if a giant had picked them up and bowled them along the ground like a ball in an alley." Nearly every house showed signs of damage. Some lost their roofs, others were tipped over or shifted off their foundations, many were smashed to the ground in splinters. The *New York Times* reported, "Half the handsome shade trees were gone—uprooted or twisted off. The lawns and streets were covered with broken timbers, glass, parts of roofs, and branches of trees. In the gardens the leaves were stripped from the corn, leaving bare stalks, nearly flat on the ground." The Dutch Reformed Church, a solid brick building erected two years earlier, was barely standing: its walls were askew, all its windows broken, and it was three feet off its foundation. "Three large beams, picked from the wreck of other buildings by the wind, were borne, end on end, against the side of the church, and went through the walls as though they had been paper instead of brick," said the *Times*. The railroad depot was demolished. Heavy planks from the freight platform were torn up and thrown hundreds of feet away. One plank, wrote the *Times*, "struck the trunk of a tree, and for a distance of ten inches was flattened out and splintered as though it had been beneath the weight of a piledriver."

Figure 24. Downtown Cherry Hill was devastated when a tornado struck the Bergen County village in July 1895, killing three and injuring hundreds. Conrad Friedman was crushed to death when his hotel collapsed on him. From the *New York Herald*, July 16, 1895.

Relief efforts began almost immediately. Firemen from Hackensack, Tenafly, Bergen, and Westwood who arrived by train worked clearing debris, demolishing dangerous buildings, and guarding personal effects. Train crews had the railroad tracks cleared within two hours. Doctors from Hackensack were soon on the scene tending the wounded, most of them injured by flying debris, and the state government sent army tents to house the homeless. Set up the day after the disaster, the Cherry Hill Tornado Relief Fund eventually raised nearly $5,000 for the victims.

On Sunday, the Reverend Duryee of the Dutch Reformed Church gathered his flock on the lawn of the wrecked building. Accompanied by a small organ salvaged from the ruins, his parishioners read scripture and sang hymns, thanking God for their deliverance.

SOURCES AND
SUGGESTIONS FOR
FURTHER READING

CHAPTER 1 — FIRES

Newark—October 27, 1836

This account of Newark's worst fire is based on news stories that appeared in the *New-Jersey Journal's* issue of November 1, 1836, and the *Newark Daily Advertiser* of October 28, 1836. Secondary sources consulted include one nineteenth-century history, Joseph Atkinson's *The History of Newark, New Jersey* (Newark: William B. Guild, 1878); and John T. Cunningham's excellent modern book, *Newark* (Newark: New Jersey Historical Society, 1966). Newark's fire followed by ten months a blaze that incinerated New York City's financial district. Gunpowder from the Brooklyn Navy Yard was used to blow up buildings in the path of the New York fire, slowing its advance. The two naval officers who volunteered for the same duty in Newark probably knew what had been achieved across the Hudson but, alas, could find no powder. The statistics in the introduction to the chapter are from *Fire in New Jersey, 2010*, a publication of the New Jersey Division of Fire Safety, New Jersey Department of Community Affairs.

Cape May City—September 5, 1856

Although Cape May County's first newspaper, the *Ocean Wave*, was founded about 1855, no issues have survived from 1856, the year of the Mount Vernon Hotel fire. Both the *Newark Daily Advertiser* and *New-York*

Daily Times, however, carried stories in their September 8, 1856, editions. The papers estimated the loss at about $150,000, none of which was insured. A twenty-thousand-gallon tank of water located in the center of one wing was designed to fight any fire that might break out but was not used, probably because the staff had been furloughed for the winter.

Cape May City—August 31, 1869

September 1, 1869, editions of the *Cape May Ocean Wave, Newark Daily Advertiser,* and *New York Times* contained extensive coverage of the fire. For further information about the growth and decline of Cape May as one of the state's most popular summer resorts, see George E. Thomas and Carl Daebley's book *Cape May, Queen of the Seaside Resorts* (Philadelphia: Art Alliance Press, 1976); and William H. McMahon, *South Jersey Towns: History and Legend* (New Brunswick, NJ: Rutgers University Press, 1973). A wider view of New Jersey's seashore resorts will be found in Harold F. Wilson's book *The Story of the Jersey Shore* (Princeton, NJ: Van Nostrand, 1964).

Cape May City—November 9, 1878

Newspaper coverage of the fire was extensive. The *New York Times* on November 10, 1878; the *Newark Daily Advertiser* and *New York Tribune* on November 11, 1878; and the weekly *Cape May Wave* on November 16, 1878, covered the blaze at great length. An article by Susan Tischler, "Cape May on Fire," dated November 1, 2003, at CapeMay.com, http://capemay.com/magazine/2003/11/cape-may-on-fire/#axzz2Twy5l3gB, contains photos of some of the hotels that burned and a map of the burned-over district. The discouraged owners of Congress Hall, their loss estimated at $125,000, reportedly intended to subdivide the site (one of the largest in Cape May) for cottage lots but reconsidered, rebuilding in fireproof brick a year later.

Newton—September 22, 1873

Stories about the Newton fire appeared in the *Newark Daily Journal*, September 23, 1873; *Newark Evening Courier*, September 22, 1873; *New York Times*, September 23 and 24, 1873; *Sussex Register*, September 25, 1873; and the *Sussex Independent*, quoted in the *Newark Star*, September 17, 1925. Other sources for the story include an article from the *New Jersey Herald*, December 23, 1962, titled "Disastrous Blaze Woke Town to Need"; *The Historical Directory of Sussex County, N.J.*, edited by Edward A. Webb (Andover, NJ: 1872); and James P. Snell's *History of Sussex and Warren Counties, New Jersey* (Philadelphia: Everts & Peck, 1881). Although there appear to be no photos of the Newton fire, townspeople long remembered the worst disaster in the community's history, inviting a delegation from Hoboken to march in the town's annual firemen's parade held seventy-eight years later (*Newark Evening News*, September 23, 1951).

Caven Point, Jersey City, Refinery Fire—May 10, 1883

Lengthy articles in the *Evening Journal* (Jersey City), *New York Herald,* and *New York Times* on May 11, 1883, detail the course of the fire.

The Standard Oil Fire, Bayonne—July 5, 1900

Visible for miles around, the Standard Oil fire was big news. Jersey City's *Evening Journal,* July 6 and 9, 1900; *Jersey City News,* July 6, 1900; *Newark Evening News,* July 6 and 7, 1900; *New York Herald,* July 6 and 7, 1900; and *New York Times,* July 5–8, 1900, carried the story. For information about the history of Bayonne and its industries, see Kathleen M. Middleton's book in the Arcadia series, *Images of America: Bayonne* (Dover, NH: Arcadia Publishing, 1995). Superintendent Wedge and family appear in the 1900 United States Census, Bayonne, Third Ward, sheet 25. A brief history of Standard Oil Company of New Jersey appears in the *Encyclopedia of New Jersey,* edited by Maxine N. Lurie and Marc Mappen (New Brunswick, NJ: Rutgers University Press, 2004). More detail can be found in *Century of Discovery: An Exxon Album,* published in 1982 by the Exxon Corporation, New York. At the time of the fire, some observers blamed the disaster on disgruntled oil yard workers, a theory quickly disproved. Labor unrest at the Bayonne refinery was long-standing, however. In June 1889, two hundred boilermakers, riveters, heaters, and helpers struck for a reduction in their day from ten to nine hours. Three years later, Hungarian workers (the *New York Times* called them "Huns") struck for higher wages, attacking other workers who refused to join them. Labor strife broke out again in May 1900, just two months before the fire. "The strikers at the Standard Oil Works, of Constable Hook, Bayonne, N.J., made a determined effort yesterday to prevent men from going to work in their places," reported the *New York Times.* "Nearly every man who attempted to enter the works was assaulted. A number of shots were fired by the workers, but no one was hit. The police and deputy sheriffs repeatedly charged the rioters, and used their clubs on them." *New York Times,* June 26, 1889; April 16, 1892; and May 6, 1900.

CHAPTER 2 — STEAMBOAT DISASTERS

New-Jersey—Camden—March 15, 1856

The loss of the *New-Jersey* was headline news in the New York, New Jersey, and Philadelphia newspapers. The *Newark Daily Advertiser,* March 17, 1856; *New-York Daily Times,* March 17, 18, and 19, 1856; and *New York Herald,* March 17, 1856, quoted at length from the *Philadelphia Evening Bulletin,* the *Inquirer,* and the *Public Ledger,* as was the custom of the time. The grand jury, whose findings were reported in full in the *New-York Daily Times* of April 8, 1856, exonerated the captain and crew, instead blaming the disaster on the steamboat's owners and Richard Fetters, whose job it was to inspect the boiler.

Isaac Newton—Fort Lee—December 5, 1863

The twin devils of high-pressure steam and wood-burning (later coal-fueled) fire chambers made steamboat travel extremely hazardous. During the early nineteenth century high-pressure (50 to 150 pounds per square inch) steam boilers gradually replaced low-pressure (7 to 10 pounds) boilers. Although more efficient, the newer steamboats were prone to disaster. Between 1810 and 1850, there were some four thousand fatalities on all U.S. rivers as a result of boiler explosions. The frequent explosions prompted

Charles Dickens to compare steamboat travel to living "on the first floor of a gun powder mill." The worst disaster on record was the explosion of the *Sultana* on April 27, 1865, near Memphis, Tennessee. The steamboat was carrying 2,400 Union prisoners of war back home when one of four boilers exploded, killing 1,700 men. In August 1852, Congress put teeth into steamboat laws by licensing all pilots and engineers and requiring inspection of all steam vessels plying federal waters. See "Gently Down the Stream: How Exploding Steamboat Boilers in the 19th Century Ignited Federal Public Welfare Legislation," a third-year paper by Gregory P. Sandukas, Harvard Law School, April 30, 2002, found at http://leda.law.harvard.edu. The *New York Herald,* December 7, 1863; *New York Times,* December 7, 8, and 9, 1863; and *New York Daily Tribune,* December 7, 1863, reported the *Isaac Newton* story. For information about the *Isaac Newton* and other steamboats of the time, see Frank Donovan's book *River Boats of America* (New York: Thomas Y. Crowell, 1966).

CHAPTER 3 — TRAIN WRECKS

Burlington—August 29, 1855

For an overview of nineteenth-century train travel, see *The Story of American Railroads* by Stewart H. Holbrook (New York: Crown Publishers, 1947); and *Train Wrecks* by Robert C. Reed (New York: Bonanza Books, 1968). Specific to New Jersey is John T. Cunningham's *Railroads in New Jersey: The Formative Years* (Andover, NJ: Afton Publishing, 1997). The Secaucus wreck was reported in the *New-York Daily Times* on December 10, 1853. The Burlington train wreck was covered by the *New-York Daily Times* in its August 30 and 31 and September 1 and 6, 1855, editions.

Hackensack Meadows—January 15, 1894

The Meadows train wreck was a page-one story in all the metropolitan newspapers. This account is based on stories that ran in the *Newark Daily Advertiser,* January 15–19, 1894; *Newark Evening News,* January 15, 16, and 17, 1894; *New York Herald,* January 16 and 17, 1894; and *New York Times,*

January 16, 17, 18, 26, and 27, February 9, and March 11, 1894. No photographs apparently exist; the *Herald* and *Advertiser* illustrated their stories with drawings made at the scene. The wreck site is within a loop of the Hackensack River just north of the point where the PATH tracks, Newark–Jersey City Turnpike, and Fish House Road come together. The Kearny Railroad Yards lie a few hundred yards to the southwest.

May's Landing—August 11, 1880

Newspaper coverage of the May's Landing wreck was comprehensive. The *Newark Daily Advertiser,* August 12, 1880; *New York Herald,* August 14, 1880; *New York Times,* August 12, 13, 14, 18, 19, and 22–25, 1880; *New York Tribune,* August 13, 1880; and *Philadelphia Inquirer,* August 13, 14, and 24, 1880, are the sources for this story. According to Edgar A. Haine, in his *Railroad Wrecks* (New York: Cornwall Books, 1993), by December 1880, the railroad company had settled eighteen death and twenty-two injury claims for $50,800, with another eight death claims in process of resolution. Haine's book covers all of the major New Jersey wrecks. For a lively account of the history of Atlantic City, see *By the Beautiful Sea* by Charles E. Funnell (New York: Alfred A. Knopf, 1975).

Absecon Island—July 30, 1896

The Improved Order of Red Men, a patriotic society founded in 1834, still exists, with three "councils" active in New Jersey. This section is based on news articles appearing in the *Newark Evening News,* July 31 and August 2 and 3, 1896; and *New York Times,* August 3, 1896.

Bordentown—February 21, 1901

The wreck of the Nellie Bly happened two and a half miles north of Bordentown. For a detailed account with photographs, see "The Crash of the Nellie Bly," a story by Mark W. Falzini, archivist, dated February 17, 2009, appearing in Archival Ramblings, an Internet post of the New Jersey State Police Museum, http://njspmuseum.blogspot.com/2009/02/it-took-80-days-for-phineas-fogg-to.html. My story is based on articles printed in the

Newark Evening News, February 22, 1901; *New York Times,* February 22 and 23, 1901; and *Trenton Times,* February 26, and March 2 and 29, 1901.

The Thoroughfare Wreck—October 28, 1906

The *Newark Evening News,* October 29, 30, and 31, 1906; and *New York Times,* October 30, 1906, covered the wreck. For further reading, I recommend John T. Cunningham's early work, *Railroading in New Jersey* (Newark: Associated Railroads of New Jersey, 1952) and the more recent *Iron Rails in the Garden State: Tales of New Jersey Railroading* by Anthony J. Bianculli (Bloomington: Indiana University Press, 2008). Three months after the accident, a further investigation revealed that although the signals showed clear, the rails were misaligned after the drawbridge had been opened and closed several times. Charges were then filed against the West Jersey Railroad for operating an unsafe bridge. Stewart, who had spent three months in jail on a charge of criminal negligence, was released.

CHAPTER 4 — SHIPWRECKS

John Minturn—South of Mantoloking—February 15, 1846

The two best books on New Jersey shipwrecks are Margaret T. Buchholz's *New Jersey Shipwrecks: 350 Years in the Graveyard of the Atlantic* (Harvey Cedars, NJ: Down the Shore Publishing, 2004); and Gary Gentile's work *Shipwrecks of New Jersey (North)* (Philadelphia: G. Gentile Productions, 2000), written from a diver's viewpoint. The Lifesaving Service is the subject of *Surfboats, Rockets, and Carronades,* written by Robert F. Bennett, commander of the U.S. Coast Guard and published in 1976 by Government Printing Office, Washington, DC. Congressman Newell's role in establishing the service is covered in Francis Bazley Lee's *New Jersey as a Colony and as a State* (New York: Publishing Society of New Jersey, 1903), vol. 4; and, more recently by John T. Cunningham, *The New Jersey Sampler* (Upper Montclair: New Jersey Almanac, 1964). Captain Stark's identification was established by consulting *The Aaron Stark Family: Seven Generations of the Descendants of Aaron Stark of Groton, Connecticut* by Charles R. Stark

(Boston: privately printed, 1927). For newspaper reports of the *Minturn's* loss, see the *Newark Daily Advertiser*, February 21, 1846; and *New York Herald*, February 17 and 18, 1846. Additional contemporary accounts from the *New York Journal of Commerce* are quoted in Mary Cable's "Damned Plague Ships and Swimming Coffins," *American Heritage* 11, no. 5 (August 1960). The Pilot's Monument in Brooklyn's Green-Wood Cemetery was erected by fellow harbor pilots in Thomas Freeborn's memory. A depiction of the *John Minturn* is carved on the front of the monument, which is decorated with a capstan and anchors. A photo of the monument can be found on the Forgotten New York website, http://forgotten-ny .com/2006/04/forgotten-tour-24-green-wood-cemetery-part-1-brooklyn.

Powhattan—Beach Haven—April 15, 1854

Besides Buchholz's and Gentile's books, much useful information will be found in *Broken Spars: New Jersey Coast Shipwrecks, 1640–1935*, by Leland Woolley Downey, published in 1983 by the Brick Township Historical Society, Brick, NJ. Anyone interested in the purgatory through which immigrants had to pass will want to read *Strangers at the Door* by Ann Novotny (Riverside, CT: Chatham Press, 1971); and "Damned Plague Ships and Swimming Coffins," an article by Mary Cable published in *American Heritage* 11, no. 5 (August 1960). Both the *New-York Daily Times* and *New York Herald* covered the *Powhattan* disaster on April 21 and 22, 1854.

New Era—Deal Beach—November 13, 1854

For reasons not clear, the loss of the *New Era* inspired more local newspaper coverage than any other nineteenth-century wreck on the Jersey shore. The *New-York Daily Times*, *New York Herald*, and *New York Daily Tribune* ran hundreds of inches of copy in their November 14, 15, and 16, 1854, editions. After others lost interest, the *Daily Times* kept at it, carrying stories about the wreck and its aftermath on November 22, 24, and 28, 1854, and January 24 and 25, 1855. Perhaps it was the obvious negligence of the ship's captain and senior officers that stirred the press and others. In an article headlined "Appalling Shipwreck of the New Era," *Monthly Nautical Magazine and Quarterly Review* 1 (April–September 1855) argued that it was "a grave question of most significant import, whether there shall, or shall not be (as at present) a remedy for such culpable recklessness as this which consigns the trusting passenger to the tender mercies of *fate*, whenever he sets foot on ship-board." Articles about the loss of the *New Era* were collected by Julius Friedrich Sachse and published by the Pennsylvania-German Society under the title *The Wreck of the Ship New Era upon the New Jersey Coast* (Lancaster, PA, 1907).

New York—North of Barnegat Inlet—December 20, 1856

The sources for this story are articles appearing in the *New-York Daily Times* and *New York Herald* on December 23 and 24, 1856. Both papers covered the disaster in considerable depth. For information about the *New York* as well as other ships of the era, see the "Palmer List of Merchant Vessels" by Michael P. Palmer at http://www.geocities.com/mppraetorius/com-ne.htm. Besides Margaret T. Buchholz's fine book, readers are directed to *Under Barnegat's Beam* by Bayard Randolph Kraft (New York: privately printed, 1960).

Vizcaya and *Cornelius Hargraves*—Off Barnegat Bay—October 30, 1890

This chapter is based on articles appearing in the *New York Herald, New York Times*, and *New York Tribune*, November 1–4, 1890. The rules of navigation are discussed in "Port and Starboard," an article in the online encyclopedia *Wikipedia*, http://en.wikipedia.org/wiki/Port_and_starboard. Most likely, the sharp prow of the *Cornelius Hargraves*, a wooden ship, cut the steel-hulled *Vizcaya* virtually in half because the stoutly built schooner was sailing fast with a heavy burden of coal below decks. The schooner had the advantage of weight and speed. For the story of the great Maine coal schooners, see the website of the Penobscot Marine Museum, http://www.penobscotmarinemuseum.org/pbho-1/ships-shipbuilding/great-coal-schooners. For a Spanish view of the collision (as well as illustrations of

Captain Cunill, other officers, and the *Vizcaya* itself), readers are directed to an article by Vincent Sanahuja titled "Cunill Francisco and the End of *Vizcaya*" that appeared in *Marine Life*, a Spanish publication accessible at http://vidamaritima.com/en/2010/11/don-francisco-cunill-y-el-fin-del -vizcaya. A drawing of the *Cornelius Hargraves* will be found at http:// www.wrecksite.eu/wreck.aspx?20308.

Delaware—Barnegat Bay—July 8, 1898

A photograph of the *Delaware* in port appears in Gary Gentile's book. Articles in the *New York Herald* and *New York Times* on July 10, 1898, are the sources of the story. Captain Ingram's post-*Delaware* adventures are recorded in the *New York Times* on June 28, 1899; and November 13, 1914.

CHAPTER 5 — NATURAL DISASTERS
The Blizzard of '88—March 11–14, 1888

David M. Ludlum's *The New Jersey Weather Book* (New Brunswick, NJ: Rutgers University Press, 1983) is the best source for historical information about New Jersey weather. *Blizzard! The Great Storm of '88* by Judd Caplovitch (Vernon, CT: VeRo Publishing, 1987) contains hundreds of fascinating photographs, some of New Jersey. Another good source is *The Blizzard of '88* by Irving Werstein (New York: Thomas Y. Crowell, 1960). Every area newspaper carried stories about the blizzard, the biggest news event of the decade. This chapter is based on stories from the *Asbury Park Journal*, March 17, 1888; *Cape May Gazette*, March 16, 1888; *Elizabeth Journal*, March 13, 1888; *Evening Journal* (Jersey City), March 12 and 13, 1888; *Hunterdon County Democrat*, March 20, 1888; *Madison Weekly Eagle*, March 16, 1888; *Monmouth Democrat*, March 15, 1888; *Mount Holly Herald*, March 17, 1888; *Newark Daily Advertiser*, March 12, 1888; *Newark Evening News*, March 14–18, 1888; *Newark Sunday Call*, March 28, 1888; *New Brunswick Times*, March 13, 1888; *New Jersey Journal*, March 13 and 14, 1888; *New York Herald*, March 14 and 15, 1888; *New York Times*, March 14 and 15, 1888; *New York Tribune*, March 14 and 17, 1888; *Paterson Morning Call*, March 14, 1888; *Perth Amboy*

Republican, March 14 and 16, 1888; *Philadelphia Inquirer,* March 14 and 16, 1888; *Plainfield Daily Press,* March 13, 1888; *Somerville Unionist Gazette,* March 15 and 22, 1888; *Stanhope Eagle,* March 14, 1888; *Sussex Register,* March 14, 1888; and *Trenton Daily State Gazette,* March 14, 1888.

The Great September Gale—September 3, 1821

In addition to Ludlum's *New Jersey Weather Book,* the reader will want to visit *Great Storms of the Jersey Shore* by Larry Savadove and Margaret Thomas Buchholz (Harvey Cedars, NJ: Down the Shore Publishing, 1993). Firsthand accounts of the 1821 hurricane are elusive. This section relies on stories appearing in the *Cape May Spray* (n.d., quoted in Ludlum); *New Brunswick Fredonian,* September 13, 1821; *New-Jersey Eagle,* September 7, 1821; *New-Jersey Journal and Elizabeth Town Gazette,* September 11, 1821; *New York Evening Post,* September 4, 1821; *Niles' Register,* September 29, 1821; Newark's *Sentinel of Freedom,* September 11, 1821; *Sussex Register* (n.d., quoted in Ludlum); and *Trenton Federalist* (n.d., quoted in the *Niles' Register*).

Statewide Hurricane—September 10–13, 1889

Ludlum's and Savadove's books, as well as articles printed in the *Cape May County Gazette,* September 15, 1889; *Jersey Journal,* September 13, 1889; *Monmouth Democrat,* September 19, 1889; *Newark Evening News,* September 10–13, 1889; *New York Times,* September 11–13, 1889; *New York Tribune,* September 12–14, 1889; *Philadelphia Inquirer,* September 12, 1889; and *Shore Press* (Asbury Park), September 13, 1889, are the sources for this story.

New Brunswick Tornado—June 19, 1835

The *New Brunswick Times* and *New York Gazette,* both June 23, 1835, and *Niles' Register,* June 27, 1835, contain stories about the tornado. As usual, Ludlum's book is invaluable.

Camden Tornado—July 26, 1860

The story is from the *Philadelphia Press,* July 27, 1860.

Camden Tornado—August 3, 1885

The *Camden Post* reported the story on August 4, 1885. The *Philadelphia Inquirer* also ran articles about the tornado on August 4–6, 1885.

Cherry Hill Tornado—July 13, 1895

According to *The New Jersey Weather Book*, again the basic source for weather information, most New Jersey tornadoes are short-lived, perhaps a few minutes at most, have narrow tracks only a few yards wide, and cover limited distances. The Camden tornado that demolished a chemical factory would have been typical except for its unusual strength. The New Brunswick tornado, second Camden tornado, and the one that demolished Cherry Hill were unusual because of the length of their tracks. The Cherry Hill tornado ended its destructive work in Woodhaven, New York, eight miles east of New York City, where it flattened buildings and killed one person. A full story of the tornado appears in the American Meteorological Society's *Monthly Weather Review* for July 1895. Newspaper articles used for this story ran in the *Newark Daily Advertiser*, July 15, 1895; *New York Herald*, July 16, 1895; *New York Times*, July 14 and 15, 1895; and *New York World*, July 15, 1895. Photos of the destruction wrought by the tornado can be found in *Musket, Anchor and Plow: The Story of River Edge, 1677–1976* (New York: Arno Press, 1976), by Naomi and George Howitt, and on the Internet. Cherry Hill is located in the northeast corner of River Edge.

INDEX

West Jersey Railroad, 153, 182
West Jersey Seashore Electric Railroad,
   87
West Long Branch Methodist Cemetery,
   119
Westwood, NJ, 191
Wildwood, NJ, 170

Williamson, Dayton, 5
Winham, Charles, 130–131
Witthaus, R. A., 116
Wolfe, Theresa, 116
Woodbury, NJ, 166
Woodward, W. W., 18–19
wreckmasters, 97–102, 111, 121

ABOUT THE AUTHOR

A Phi Beta Kappa graduate of Rutgers University, Columbia University, and Rutgers School of Law, Alan A. Siegel is a practicing attorney in Chatham with an abiding interest in state and local history. *Disaster! Stories of Destruction and Death in Nineteenth-Century New Jersey* is his tenth book and the third published by Rutgers University Press. The New Jersey League of Historical Societies and the County of Somerset, where he lives, have recognized his work.